CLOSE YET FRAGMENTED

UNDERSTANDING AND NAVIGATING DISORGANIZED ATTACHMENT

VALERIE GRAY

For my Wonderful Family

To heal is to touch with love that which we previously touched with fear.

— STEPHEN LEVINE

CONTENTS

INTRODUCTION

THE COMPLEX WORLD OF ATTACHMENT

Human relationships are an intricate dance shaped by unseen forces that frequently operate below our conscious awareness. Attachment theory, for example, emphasizes the formative nature of early human connections. The bonds we form with our primary caregivers set the tone for a lifetime of relationships from the moment we are born.

Attachment, however, is not a one-dimensional concept. It has complexities, variations, and nuances. Once relegated to the dusty shelves of academic discourse, this theory has made its way into mainstream discourse, highlighting its relevance and significance in our daily lives. It has shed light on the pathways of our interpersonal dynamics, demonstrating how patterns established early in life can reverberate throughout our lives.

Attachment theory has its origins in the twentieth century, with pioneers such as John Bowlby and Mary Ainsworth leading the charge. Their seminal work established the foundation for our modern understanding of attachment, emphasizing the importance of a secure foundation from which individuals can explore the world. A plethora of research has sprung up as a result of this foundation, broadening the lens through which we view human connections.

These discoveries have far-reaching implications. They illuminate not only the bond between an infant and caregiver but also our adult relationships, shaping our roles as partners, parents, and friends. Attachment is more than a theoretical construct; it influences the emotional, cognitive, and social aspects of our existence, intertwining with our very identity.

Different attachment styles emerge in this vast universe, each with its own flavor and set of implications. They serve as blueprints for our interactions, expectations, and emotional responses. As we progress through this book, we'll embark on a journey through the intricate maze of these attachment styles, focusing in particular on one that frequently eludes understanding: disorganized attachment.

DISORGANIZED ATTACHMENT: AN OVERVIEW

Because of its inherent paradox, disorganized attachment stands out in the pantheon of attachment styles. Disorganized attachment, in contrast to other styles that present a consistent (though possibly maladaptive) approach to relationships, is a whirlwind of conflicting impulses. At its core, it is a strategy devoid of strategy, characterized by a tumultuous interplay of avoidance and anxiety.

This type of attachment often emerges from situations where the caregiver is both a source of comfort and fear in early childhood landscapes. This creates a crippling conundrum for the child, who is drawn to the caregiver for solace while also fearful of potential harm or rejection. Confusion, uncertainty, and a sense of being trapped in an emotional quagmire are all fostered in such an environment.

The resulting adult behaviors can be diverse and unpredictable. Individuals with disorganized attachment oscillate between relational extremes, ranging from intense dependence to stark detachment. Their inner world is similarly chaotic, with feelings of unworthiness alternating with an overinflated sense of self.

This upheaval is not limited to romantic relationships. It pervades friendships, familial bonds, and even professional interactions. The uncertainty and volatility inherent in disorganized attachment affect every aspect of an individual's life, making it an important area of investigation and comprehension.

Nonetheless, despite its complexities, there is hope. The first step toward healing is awareness. We can chart a course toward healthier, more secure relational dynamics by demystifying disorganized attachment and delving deeply into its origins, manifestations, and implications. This book aspires to be a compass on that journey, shedding light on the dark corners of disorganized attachment and providing pathways to change.

BRIEF RECAP OF AVOIDANT AND ANXIOUS ATTACHMENT

Before digging deeper into disorganized attachment, consider its more well-known counterparts, avoidant and anxious attachment. These two attachment patterns, like all others, have their origins in early interactions with caregivers and serve as a blueprint for later relational behaviors.

Avoidant attachment, characterized by emotional distance and self-reliance, develops in the context of a consistently unmet or dismissed emotional need. Individuals with this personality style frequently prioritize independence, keeping others at a distance to protect themselves from the pain of rejection or unmet needs.

Anxious attachment, on the other hand, is the result of inconsistent caregiving. The child is exposed to nurturing moments interspersed with neglect or unpredictability. This results in heightened sensitivity to relational dynamics, an ongoing fear of abandonment, and a clinging nature in relationships.

Both of these styles, despite their differences in manifestation, share common underpinnings. They are defense mechanisms that evolved in response to early relational environments. Individuals attempt to navigate the perilous waters of human connection by distancing themselves or clinging desperately, seeking safety, security, and validation.

Understanding these styles is critical, not only as standalone entities but also in comparison to disorganized attachment. While avoidant and anxious attachments have distinct patterns, disorganized attachment is a labyrinth of both, with deeper layers of trauma and confusion layered on top. While focusing on disorganized attachment, this book frequently draws parallels and contrasts with these other attachment styles, providing a comprehensive picture of the attachment spectrum.

THE REAL-LIFE IMPACT OF DISORGANIZED ATTACHMENT

The consequences of disorganized attachment are not limited to textbooks or therapy sessions. They impact countless people's daily lives, shaping their experiences, decisions, and overall life trajectories. Its influence extends from the intimacy of personal relationships to the broad strokes of professional and social interactions.

One of the most important implications concerns relationships. Those with disorganized attachment are frequently on an emotional rollercoaster, alternating between a deep yearning for closeness and a paralyzing fear of it. This push-pull dynamic can strain relationships, resulting in cycles of insecurity, breakups, and reunions.

Friendships, in addition to romantic relationships, bear the brunt of this attachment style. Trust, the foundation of any healthy friendship, is frequently a battleground. The person may oscillate between being overly trusting to the point of naivety and being overly guarded, shutting out even those who mean well.

Team dynamics, leadership, and even basic interpersonal interactions pose challenges in the professional sphere. Disorganized attachment's unpredictability can lead to misunderstandings, conflicts, and, at times, missed opportunities. Internal strife frequently spills over, affecting decision-making, communication, and collaboration.

Additionally, the inner experience of someone with disorganized attachment can be a whirlwind of self-doubt, confusion, and emotional pain. Memories of past traumas, unresolved feelings toward caregivers, and a persistent feeling of being 'unmoored' can be mentally and emotionally draining.

However, it is critical to remember that these implications, while difficult, are not insurmountable. Individuals can navigate their way to healthier attachment patterns, richer relationships, and a more harmonious inner world with understanding, support, and the right interventions.

WHY THIS BOOK MATTERS

Why should this book be on your shelf, given the vast amount of literature on human psychology, relationships, and personal growth? The answer is found in the delicate interplay of relevance, depth, and actionable insights that it provides. Despite its significant impact, disorganized attachment remains a misunderstood and frequently overlooked area. This book aims to fill that void.

This book appeals to a wide range of readers by providing a comprehensive examination of disorganized attachment. Whether you identify with this attachment style, a loved one who is trying to understand, or a professional in the field, the insights provided here are designed to resonate, educate, and empower.

Furthermore, the subject of attachment is not merely academic; it is deeply personal. Our attachment styles shape our decisions, reactions, and even the lens through which we see the world. This book provides readers with a mirror, a tool for introspection, and a beacon of hope by delving into the complexities of disorganized attachment.

Beyond understanding, the book emphasizes actionable strategies. Knowledge, while powerful on its own, becomes exponentially more powerful when combined with tools for change. The book transforms from a source of information to a transformational roadmap through exercises, real-life examples, and practical advice.

The stories on these pages also highlight the strength of human resilience. They emphasize the idea that, regardless of past traumas or current difficulties, healing and growth are always possible. This book is an ode to that potential, a testament to the indomitable human spirit, which can overcome, evolve, and thrive with the right support.

PERSONAL STORIES: LIVING WITH DISORGANIZED ATTACHMENT

Narratives have a special power. They immerse us in someone else's world, allowing us to see through their eyes, feel their emotions, and walk a mile in their shoes. The personal stories of people who have lived and continue to live with disorganized attachment enrich this book. These stories, both heartbreaking and inspiring, add depth and authenticity to the discussion.

These individuals provide a firsthand account of the challenges and triumphs associated with disorganized attachment by sharing their journeys. They talk about the agony of childhood traumas, the confusion of opposing impulses, and the hope that comes from understanding and intervention. The theoretical aspects of disorganized attachment come to life through their voices, grounding them in the tangible realities of everyday life.

Furthermore, these stories serve as a beacon of hope. They emphasize the idea that change is possible no matter how difficult the journey is. Many people have charted a course toward more secure attachment patterns, meaningful relationships, and inner peace through therapy, introspection, and sheer resilience.

These stories also serve as a bridge, connecting readers to a larger community of people who have had similar experiences. They remind us that we are not alone in our struggles and that countless others around the world face similar challenges, dreams, and aspirations. There is solace, strength, and the promise of a brighter tomorrow in this shared journey.

The stories in these pages also emphasize the value of compassion, both for oneself and for others. They teach us that behind every erratic behavior and every push-pull dynamic, there is a story to be told, often one of pain, longing, and a deep desire for connection. Through these narratives, the book invites readers to view the world through a more empathetic lens, fostering understanding and connecting people.

RESEARCH AND REALITY

Balancing personal narratives is one of the research pillars upon which this book is built. Disorganized attachment, like all psychological constructs, is best understood by combining empirical evidence and real-world application. This book strives to provide a balanced mix of the two, ensuring that the content is both scientifically sound and deeply relatable.

The book provides a comprehensive overview of disorganized attachment, drawing on the most recent findings in psychology, neuroscience, and therapeutic interventions. The content is founded on rigorous research and presented in an approachable manner, from its origins to its manifestations and implications.

However, research conducted in isolation can often feel abstract. The book bridges this gap by interspersing empirical findings with real-life examples, case studies, and narratives. This intertwining of data and human stories ensures that, while scientifically sound, the content resonates on a deeply personal level.

Additionally, the research presented here is dynamic. Attachment theory, like all fields of science, is constantly evolving. New discoveries are made, paradigms shift, and our understanding grows. While grounded in current knowledge, this book also hints at future possibilities, encouraging readers to remain curious, open-minded, and engaged in the ever-evolving world of attachment research.

The combination of research and reality, science and stories, distinguishes this book. It takes readers on an exploration journey, where hard facts collide with human experiences to weave a tapestry of understanding that is both intellectually stimulating and emotionally enriching.

THE IMPORTANCE OF HEALING AND GROWTH

The theme of healing and growth is central to the narrative of this book. While disorganized attachment presents a number of difficulties, it is not a life sentence. Individuals can move toward more secure attachment patterns, forging richer, more fulfilling relationships, with understanding, intervention, and a commitment to personal growth.

Healing from past wounds is a journey that is often difficult but always rewarding. It necessitates confronting painful memories, challenging ingrained beliefs, and forging new, healthier patterns of interpersonal interaction. This book serves as a guide along the way, providing insights, tools, and strategies to aid in the healing process.

However, healing is not solely an individual endeavor. It has a positive impact on families, communities, and even future generations. Individuals who heal form stronger bonds, allowing children to form secure attachments and breaking the cycle of trauma and dysfunction.

This book also advocates for growth, which is a close ally of healing. It's the promise of progress, the desire to be the best versions of ourselves. The book examines avenues for personal growth, whether in relationships, self-awareness, or overall emotional well-being, through the lens of disorganized attachment.

The story of healing and growth is ultimately one of hope. It demonstrates the human spirit's ability to overcome, adapt, and thrive. Readers are invited to embark on this transformative journey through the pages of this book, tapping into their innate potential and charting a course toward a brighter, more connected future.

HOW TO NAVIGATE THIS BOOK

Navigating the complex world of disorganized attachment can be daunting. However, this thoughtfully structured book aims to make this journey accessible, enlightening, and enriching. It offers readers a systematic exploration of the subject by dividing it into distinct sections, each delving into a specific facet of disorganized attachment.

Begin with the fundamental concepts, immersing yourself

in the fundamentals of attachment theory. As you progress, delve deeper into the nuances of disorganized attachment, learning about its causes, manifestations, and consequences. Engage with personal narratives along the way, allowing them to add depth and color to theoretical constructs.

The book's final sections are devoted to the themes of healing and growth. Use the exercises, reflections, and tools provided to facilitate personal transformation to engage with them actively. Remember to take your time as you navigate these pages. Understanding and healing are deeply personal journeys, and it's critical to move at a pace that feels right for you.

Finally, use this book as a companion, not just a source of information. Revisit sections, participate in exercises, and consider the insights as you travel through the landscapes of your own life. Allow it to serve as a beacon, guiding you to greater understanding, healing, and growth.

WHAT'S AHEAD: A JOURNEY OF SELF-DISCOVERY AND HEALING

You're not just consuming information when you turn the pages; you're embarking on a journey. A journey that promises increased self-awareness, more meaningful relationships, and a life full of meaning, connection, and growth. The journey may be difficult at times, filled with painful memories and harsh realities, but the destination is one of hope, healing, and trans-formation.

Allow this book to be your guide along the way, illuminating the paths of understanding, providing tools for change, and sharing stories of resilience and triumph. Allow it to remind you of your inherent potential to heal, grow, and evolve, regardless of past traumas or current challenges.

Remember that this is a shared journey as you delve deeper into the world of disorganized attachment. Countless others around the world are walking similar paths in search of understanding, solace, and transformation. Allow this sense of community to strengthen you, reminding you that you are not alone in your quest.

Above all, go into this adventure with an open heart and mind. Allow curiosity to be your guide, compassion to be your light, and hope to be your constant companion. Because the promise of a life richer in connection, understanding, and fulfillment awaits at the end of this path. Welcome to this life-changing voyage of self-discovery and healing.

THE ORIGINS OF DISORGANIZED ATTACHMENT

EARLY CHILDHOOD EXPERIENCES

*O*ur attachment patterns are built on our first interactions with the world. We begin a delicate dance with our primary caregivers the moment we are born, one that shapes our understanding of safety, connection, and love. Early childhood is a time of rapid physical and emotional development, which makes us extremely sensitive to our surroundings.

Many people associate their early experiences with warmth, consistency, and security. Positive interactions are the foundation of secure attachment. For others, however, early childhood may be rife with inconsistency, unpredictability, and even trauma, laying the groundwork for disorganized attachment patterns.

The term 'disorganized' captures the essence of these early experiences in the realm of attachment theory. It expresses the perplexity that occurs when a child's source of comfort is also a source of fear. Consider seeking solace from a caregiver who is also a source of distress. This perplexing dynamic confounds a child's innate desire for safety and connection, resulting in erratic and contradictory behavior.

It's critical to remember that these patterns are adaptive as we dive deeper into the origins of disorganized attachment. They emerge as a child's best attempt to navigate a perplexing, frequently dangerous environment. These strategies, which arose out of necessity, solidify over time, shaping interactions, expectations, and the very fabric of one's emotional world.

THE ROLE OF CAREGIVERS

Primary caregivers are crucial in shaping a child's attachment style. They serve as the initial mirror, reflecting back to the child their worthiness of love, their place in the world, and the predictability of their environment. The clarity and consistency of this reflection, as well as its distorted and erratic nature, have a significant impact on the emergence of attachment patterns.

Caregivers frequently exhibit inconsistent behaviors in cases of disorganized attachment. They may alternate between being nurturing and inaccessible or threatening and comforting. Because of this inconsistency, the child is perpetually uncertain about how to elicit care or safety.

Furthermore, some caregivers may carry unresolved trauma wounds that inadvertently spill into their parenting. Their own unmet emotional needs and unresolved issues can lead to confusing or even frightening behaviors in the child. In such situations, the child is faced with the difficulty of seeking comfort from the very person who instills fear.

Caregivers' role in fostering disorganized attachment is not about assigning blame. It recognizes the complicated interplay of past traumas, current challenges, and the overwhelming demands of parenting. Despite their best intentions, many caregivers struggle with their own emotional issues, affecting their ability to provide consistent, nurturing care.

It is, however, a call to action. Recognizing the profound impact of early caregiving on a child's emotional blueprint highlights the importance of healing, intervention, and support for caregivers as well as their children.

GENETICS AND ATTACHMENT

While early experiences and caregiver behaviors are important in shaping attachment patterns, genetics also plays a role in this complex puzzle. Attachment styles, like most aspects of human behavior, emerge from a dance between nature and nurture. Experiences fine-tune these predispositions, leading to specific outcomes. Genetics set the stage, providing a range of potentialities.

Recent behavioral genetics research suggests that certain genetic markers may be linked to susceptibility to environmental influences. This means that some people may be more sensitive to their caregiving environments, whether positive or negative.

However, it is crucial to approach the genetic basis of attachment with caution. Genetics do not determine fate. Instead, they offer a variety of possibilities that are then shaped and molded by experiences. Attachment style genetic predispositions can be thought of as tendencies, not certainties, influenced by the richness and complexity of human interactions.

Furthermore, the field of epigenetics sheds light on how experiences can influence gene expression. Environmental factors can turn certain genes on or off, including early care-giving experiences, influencing behaviors, tendencies, and overall health.

Essentially, the link between genetics and attachment demonstrates the interaction of biology and experience. It emphasizes the idea that, while we are born with certain tendencies, it is our interactions, relationships, and environments that shape these tendencies into discernible attachment patterns.

TRAUMATIC EVENTS AND THEIR IMPACT

Trauma, particularly in the formative years, can have a signifi-cant impact on the emergence of attachment patterns. Trau-matic events disrupt the child's sense of safety, predictability, and trust in the world, which frequently results in disorganized attachment behaviors. These occurrences can range from overt abuses, neglect, or witnessing violence to more subtle yet equally disruptive experiences such as emotional unavailability or inconsistent caregiving.

When a child is traumatized, their primary motivation is to seek comfort and safety, which they usually find from their caregivers. However, if the caregiver is the source of the trauma or is ill-equipped to provide solace, the child is in a difficult situation. Their innate desire for connection clashes with their desire to protect themselves from further harm.

This push-pull dynamic, which developed as a result of traumatic experiences, is at the heart of disorganized attach-ment. The child exhibits erratic behavior, sometimes seeking and sometimes resisting closeness, reflecting their internal chaos and confusion.

Moreover, trauma, particularly when it is repeated, can have an impact on brain development. Emotional regulation, threat detection, and social interactions may develop in different ways, reinforcing disorganized attachment behaviors. The body's stress response systems may also become dysregulated, resulting in increased reactivity or numbness, compounding the difficulties.

Recognizing that trauma's impact on attachment is not irreversible is critical. Both children and adults can navigate the aftereffects of trauma with timely intervention, understanding, and support, progressing toward more secure attachment patterns and overall emotional well-being.

THE BRAIN AND DISORGANIZED ATTACHMENT

Our most complex and intricate organ, the brain, plays a critical role in shaping and reinforcing attachment patterns. Early experiences, particularly those involving caregiving and attachment, impact brain development, particularly in areas related to emotion regulation, social interactions, and stress response.

Individuals with disorganized attachment frequently exhibit heightened reactivity to perceived threats. This is a byproduct of early environments in which unpredictability and potential danger were the norm. This increased reactivity can become ingrained over time, causing difficulties with emotional regulation, impulse control, and social interactions.

Also, those with disorganized attachment may have underdeveloped or disrupted neural pathways associated with comfort and safety. The inconsistent nature of early caregiving experiences, in which the source of comfort was also a potential threat, perplexes the brain's understanding of safety and connection.

Recent advancements in neuroimaging have opened a window into the brains of people who have disorganized attachment. Brain activation patterns, particularly in the amygdala (associated with threat detection) and the prefrontal cortex (associated with emotional regulation and executive functions), provide insights into the neural underpinnings of this attachment style.

The brain's plasticity, on the other hand, provides hope. The brain can change and adapt with the right interventions, therapeutic techniques, and supportive environments. Individuals can move toward more secure attachment patterns and healthier relational dynamics by forging new pathways and strengthening old ones.

CULTURAL INFLUENCES

While the fundamental concepts of attachment theory are universal, cultural differences have a significant impact on how they manifest and are interpreted. Different cultures have different caregiving practices, child-rearing expectations, and beliefs about the nature of relationships, all of which influence attachment patterns.

Practices that appear distant or uninvolved to outsiders may be normative and even desirable in certain cultures. For example, fostering independence may be more important than closeness, or communal caregiving may take precedence over the nuclear family model. While these cultural practices differ, they are not inherently harmful to attachment. However, when they intersect with inconsistency, unpredictability, or trauma, the risk of disorganized attachment increases.

Likewise, cultural differences in interpreting behaviors associated with disorganized attachment may exist. What one culture considers signs of distress or confusion may be considered normative or even adaptive by another.

It is also critical to recognize the impact of cultural traumas on attachment patterns, such as colonization, war, displacement, or systemic oppression. Such collective traumas can have a long-term impact on caregiving practices and attachment outcomes.

It is critical to approach the subject with cultural sensitivity when attempting to understand the origins of disorganized attachment. Recognizing the diversity of caregiving practices, valuing different relational norms, and recognizing the profound impact of cultural traumas all contribute to a more holistic, nuanced understanding of attachment dynamics.

LONG-TERM CONSEQUENCES

Disorganized attachment, rooted in early experiences, does not fade with time. Instead, it frequently solidifies, influencing a wide range of life domains. Disorganized attachment can have an impact on everything from interpersonal relationships to self-perception, emotional regulation to professional interactions.

Individuals who have disorganized attachment frequently struggle with internal contradictions. They may yearn for closeness but fear it; they may seek independence but feel lost without it. Internal conflicts can manifest as volatile relationships, trust issues, and difficulty navigating intimacy.

Early experiences that encourage disorganized attachment frequently result in a negative internal working model. Individuals may regard themselves as unlovable, others as unpredictable or dangerous, and the world as a place of chaos and uncertainty. These unconscious beliefs shape expectations, interactions, and overall life trajectories.

The physical consequences of disorganized attachment cannot be underestimated. Chronic stress and increased threat reactivity associated with this attachment style can have a negative impact on physical health, increasing the risk of conditions such as cardiovascular disease, immune disorders, and metabolic syndromes.

However, becoming aware of these long-term consequences is the first step toward recovery. Recognizing the pervasiveness of disorganized attachment, both emotionally and physically, underscores the importance of intervention, support, and therapeutic efforts.

DISORGANIZED VS. ORGANIZED ATTACHMENT

The world of attachment is complex, with a wide range of patterns reflecting the variety of human experiences. Disorganized attachment, at one end of the spectrum, is characterized by inconsistency, unpredictability, and internal contradictions. Secure, avoidant, and anxious attachment styles are on the other end of the spectrum.

While disorganized attachment patterns emerge in chaotic environments where the source of comfort is also a potential threat, organized attachment patterns are more predictable. For example, secure attachment results from consistent, nurturing caregiving, which leads to a positive view of oneself, others, and the world. Avoidant attachment, on the other hand, develops in situations where emotional needs are frequently dismissed or overlooked. Anxious attachment is caused by inconsistent caregiving, in which the child is unsure of their caregiver's availability or responsiveness.

However, it is critical to recognize that, while these categories are useful for understanding and intervention, they are not rigid boxes. They provide a framework for understanding the complex web of human interactions and emotional landscapes. Individuals may exhibit multiple attachment style tendencies as a result of factors such as current relationships, life stages, or recent experiences.

Also, the attachment journey is one of flux and change. Individuals can move along this spectrum with awareness, support, and intervention, moving from disorganized or insecure patterns to more secure, healthy relational dynamics.

COMMON MISCONCEPTIONS

Misconceptions abound in the realm of disorganized attachment, as they do in any complex psychological concept. One common misconception is that disorganized attachment is a life sentence, and that early experiences forever dictate future relational dynamics. While early experiences are important, the ability to change, grow, and adapt remains throughout life.

Another common misconception is that disorganized attachment is caused solely by overt trauma or abuse. While traumatic experiences can contribute to this attachment style, other factors such as inconsistent caregiving, unresolved traumas in caregivers, or genetic predispositions also play a role.

Pathologizing disorganized attachment as a 'disorder' rather than an adaptive response to early challenges is also common. Labeling it as such can stigmatize people, overshadowing their resilience, strengths, and healing capacity.

Furthermore, there is a widespread misconception that disorganized attachment is the fault of parents or primary caregivers. While caregiving practices have a significant impact on attachment patterns, it is critical to recognize the plethora of factors at work, such as the caregiver's own attachment histories, current life challenges, and systemic issues.

Demystifying these misconceptions is crucial. It fosters understanding, reduces stigma, and creates a foundation for effective interventions, support, and healing. It's a call to look at disorganized attachment with compassion, curiosity, and hope rather than judgment or blame.

REAL-LIFE CASE STUDIES

When viewed through the lens of real-life stories, the world of disorganized attachment comes to life. These diverse and poignant narratives provide a window into people's lived experiences, illuminating the nuances, challenges, and triumphs associated with this attachment style.

Consider Aisha, who grew up in a volatile household. Her father, who was dealing with his own unresolved traumas, alternated between nurturing and being explosively angry. Her mother was emotionally distant because she was overwhelmed by life's demands. Aisha's world was unpredictable, and seeking comfort often resulted in more distress. She found herself in a series of volatile relationships as an adult, mirroring the chaos of her childhood. However, through therapy, she was able to unpack her attachment patterns, paving the way for healing and healthier relationships.

Or Tony, who, despite growing up in what appeared to be a 'normal' family, displayed signs of disorganized attachment. Further investigation revealed that, while there was no obvious trauma, his caregivers' emotional availability was inconsistent. Their own relationship issues erupted, creating an environment of subtle yet pervasive unpredictability. Tony's struggled with trust issues as an adult, frequently pushing away those he cared about. However, a supportive relationship became a catalyst for his journey of understanding and transformation.

These and other stories highlight the complexities of disorganized attachment. They remind us that behind the labels and theories are real people with struggles, strengths, and the ability to change. They emphasize the importance of empathy, support, and therapeutic interventions in reshaping attachment narratives.

SYMPTOMS AND CHARACTERISTICS

RECOGNIZING DISORGANIZED ATTACHMENT IN CHILDREN

*D*isorganized attachment, rooted in early life experiences, frequently manifests vividly during childhood. Recognizing and responding to these warning signs is critical for early intervention and support.

Children with disorganized attachment have inconsistent behaviors. They may approach their caregiver for comfort, but they may resist or pull away once there. This approach-avoidance dance reflects their internal conflict: they seek safety and comfort from the very figure who distresses them.

The freezing behavior is another telling sign. When confronted with distress or uncertainty, these children may experience a brief period of emotional and physical 'stuckness,' reflecting their internal turmoil. This is frequently accompanied by a dazed or dissociated appearance, indicating internal disconnection.

Children with disorganized attachment may exhibit repetitive, strange, or even aggressive behaviors during play. Their play narratives can be chaotic, with no clear storyline or themes of helplessness or danger.

These children may also exhibit a heightened startle response, indicating hypervigilance. Living in an unpredictable world has trained their nervous system to be hypervigilant, making them reactive to even minor stimuli.

They are also known to engage in role-reversal behavior. They may become overly protective or caregiving, attempting to 'parent' their caregiver as a manifestation of their unmet emotional needs and desire for stability.

Finally, it is critical to recognize the variation in these symptoms. The manifestation of disorganized attachment can vary depending on the child's environment, temperament, and other factors, necessitating a nuanced, individualized understanding.

THE AMBIVALENCE OF ATTACHMENT

The core of disorganized attachment is ambivalence – a confusing blend of opposing desires and emotions. Children with this attachment style struggle with the paradox of seeking comfort from the same source that causes distress.

On the one hand, their innate biological drive pushes them to their caregiver for safety and nourishment. This survival instinct has been deeply ingrained in our evolutionary history, driving us toward those who can provide protection.

A conflict arises when this source of safety is also a source of fear or unpredictability. The child wants to approach but is also repulsed, resulting in typical approach-avoidance behaviors. This ambivalence is deeply emotional as well as behavioral. Love and longing become entwined with fear, distrust, or resentment. It's like navigating a maze with no clear path, which causes increased distress and confusion.

Unfortunately, this ambiguity is not limited to the caregiver-child dynamic. It frequently spills over into other relationships, laying the groundwork for future relational challenges.

Ambivalence is the emotional language of disordered attachment. Recognizing it provides insights into the inner world of the child, illuminating their struggles and needs.

PHYSICAL RESPONSES AND BEHAVIORS

Disorganized attachment has an emotional impact but also manifests physically, reflecting the profound mind-body interconnectedness. Children with disorganized attachment may experience somatic symptoms such as stomach aches or headaches as a result of their internal distress. Their bodies become the canvas for their emotions because they lack the language or awareness to articulate them.

Their posture may be slouched or defensive, indicating caution or anticipation of a threat. As previously stated, their hyper-vigilance is heightened by a heightened startle response. Sleep disorders are common. Sleep, which requires vulnerability and safety, can be difficult. These children may experience nightmares, night sweats, or insomnia, making sleep difficult.

They may also engage in self-soothing behaviors such as

rocking, thumb-sucking, or hair-twirling. Without consistent external comfort, they turn inward, attempting to calm their agitated nervous system.

It's also not uncommon for them to act aggressively. This aggression, frequently misinterpreted, is less about hostility and more about internal chaos, a way of communicating distress or seeking control. It is critical to understand these physical manifestations. It provides observable, tangible insights into their internal world, paving the way for compassionate interventions.

EMOTIONAL TURMOIL AND CONFUSION

Children with disorganized attachment have a tumultuous emotional landscape. Their internal world, riddled with contradictions and chaos, frequently mirrors their external environment.

They may experience intense, erratic emotions. Their emotional world can be a roller-coaster ride, ranging from profound sadness to rage, paralyzing fear to fleeting joy.

Emotional regulation difficulties are common. They struggle to manage their intense feelings without consistent external regulation from caregivers, resulting in emotional outbursts or shutdowns. These children frequently struggle with issues of trust. The very figures intended to instill a sense of safety and trust have caused confusion, making trust a difficult endeavor.

Even in the presence of their caregivers, they may experience feelings of abandonment. This is about more than just physical presence; it is also about emotional availability. Caregiving inconsistency makes them feel alone, even when they are surrounded.

They may experience feelings of shame or guilt. Because they misunderstand their own behaviors and emotions, they may internalize blame, believing they are flawed or unworthy.

Essentially, their emotional world is like navigating a storm without a compass. The unpredictability of the outside world becomes internalized, making emotions intimidating and over-whelming.

RELATIONSHIPS AND SOCIAL STRUGGLES

Children with disorganized attachment face significant rela-tional challenges. Because the foundation of their attachment - their primary relationship - is shaky, it impacts their broader social world.

They may have difficulty forming close friendships. Their primary caregiver's ambivalence spills over, making trust, inti-macy, and consistent connection difficult. Their friendships may be volatile as well, reflecting the chaos of their primary attachment. They may switch between clinging and distancing, intense attachment and abrupt disengagement.

Play, a primary mode of communication in childhood, might be affected. They may engage in aggressive play, have difficulty sharing, or prefer solitary play to avoid the unpre-dictability of peer interactions. Understanding social cues can be difficult. Because they live in a world where the most basic cues (from caregivers) are inconsistent, they may misread or misinterpret social signals from peers.

They may also have difficulties with authority figures such as teachers or coaches. These figures meant to provide direction and structure, may be perceived as threatening or confusing, reflecting their primary attachment dynamics.

It is important to remember, however, that these children are not inherently 'anti-social' or 'difficult.' Their actions are adaptive reactions to their inability to find stability in a world of relational unpredictability.

IMPACT ON SELF-WORTH AND IDENTITY

Children with disorganized attachment frequently have a fragile self-concept. Their identity and sense of worth can be tainted by confusion and self-doubt due to their attachment experiences.Because they internalized their caregivers' inconsistency, they may perceive themselves as unpredictable, unworthy, or flawed. They might wonder, "Am I loveable?" or "Am I deserving of care?"

This underlying self-doubt may overshadow their accomplishments or competencies. Even when they achieve success, they may find it difficult to internalize positive feedback or believe in their own abilities. Their sense of self can be shattered. Inconsistency in their external world can lead to inconsistency in their internal world, in which they struggle to maintain a stable sense of self.

Shame can be a significant part of their self-concept. They may internalize blame if they misunderstand their emotions or behaviors, leaving them feeling inherently bad or damaged.

It's critical to remember that their shaky self-esteem isn't a reflection of their inherent worth or abilities. It's a reflection of their early experiences, and it can be rebuilt with understanding and support.

BEHAVIORAL PATTERNS IN ADULTHOOD

While rooted in childhood, disorganized attachment casts long shadows on adulthood. Early behavioral patterns continue to have an impact on adult relationships, self-perception, and coping mechanisms. Adults who have a history of disorganized attachment may oscillate between relationship styles, appearing avoidant at times, anxious at others, or a confusing blend of both.

Their approach to intimacy can be characterized by ambiguity. They may crave closeness but fear it, resulting in patterns of intense involvement followed by abrupt withdrawal. Trust issues rooted in their childhood can pervade their adult relationships. They may be hypervigilant, always on the lookout for betrayal, or they may overshare, desperately seeking validation.

Childhood coping mechanisms, such as dissociation, may persist. In times of high stress or conflict, they may emotionally 'check out,' a protective strategy learned early on. It's also not uncommon for them to struggle with identity issues, such as having a consistent sense of self or feeling unworthy or self-doubt.

However, it is critical to remember that the past influences but does not dictate the present. These patterns can be recognized, understood, and transformed with awareness, support, and therapeutic interventions.

EFFECTS ON PARENTING

Parenting can be especially difficult for those who have disorganized attachment. Caregiving, which is meant to be instinctual and nurturing, can become a minefield of triggers and insecurities. They may struggle to provide consistent care. Their own experiences with inconsistency may make it difficult for them to provide predictable care, resulting in patterns of over-involvement followed by withdrawal.

Their child's emotional needs can be upsetting. When confronted with their child's emotional displays, they may become overwhelmed or distressed, echoing their own unmet needs. Role reversal patterns can emerge. They may rely on their child for emotional support or validation, blurring the lines of caregiving.

Their fear of danger, based on their own experiences, may cause them to be overly protective or concerned about their child's safety or well-being.

However, the journey of parenting provides a significant opportunity for healing. They can re-experience and reshape their attachment narrative while caring for others, breaking the cycle, and forging a new path of connection and understanding.

PERSONAL STORIES: LIVING WITH THE SYMPTOMS

Individuals' lived experiences with disorganized attachment can be both heartbreaking and enlightening. Their personal narratives reveal not only their individual struggles, but also their resilience, strength, and determination.

Samantha's Fluctuating Bonds

Samantha, a 28-year-old graphic designer, describes her relationships as an emotional roller coaster. She describes how the first stage of any relationship is euphoric, marked by a deep desire to be close and an insatiable desire to connect. However, as relationships progress, a cloud of doubt and fear descends.

Samantha recalls an incident involving her former

boyfriend, Mark. They had planned a weekend getaway, which she had eagerly anticipated. However, as the date approached, she became terrified of being abandoned and, in a panic, canceled the trip. Her yearning for closeness, followed by an intense fear of intimacy, left her isolated and frequently desolate. Samantha's story paints a moving picture of the internal conflict between a yearning for connection and an overwhelming fear of getting too close.

David's Parenting Conundrum

David's story is one of love, bewilderment, and perseverance. Every action he takes as a devoted father to his 6-year-old daughter, Emily, is motivated by deep love. Nonetheless, he speaks of moments when he is gripped by inexplicable fear and doubt. While watching Emily play in the park one evening, a sudden thought struck him: "What if I'm not good enough for her?" "What if I end up emotionally hurting her?"

These moments of self-doubt, which stem from his own traumatic childhood experiences, cause him to be overly protective, resulting in disagreements with his partner about parenting styles. David's journey demonstrates how unresolved disorganized attachment can manifest in parental concerns, even when the intention is pure love.

The Emotional Tornado of Leila

Leila, a lively university lecturer with a penchant for poetry, tells a story full of contrasts. On one hand, her emotional world is rich, deep, and intense, making her an empathetic and passionate person. This same depth, however, is frequently her Achilles' heel.

Leila describes how a simple comment from a coworker or a missed call from a friend can send her into an emotional tailspin. She describes the experience as "drowning in an ocean of emotions without a lifejacket." The highs are thrilling, but the lows are deeply disorienting. Leila's journey exemplifies the emotional turmoil of disorganized attachment while also highlighting her incredible resilience and determination to achieve equilibrium.

These stories, taken together, serve as a poignant reminder of the complex and multifaceted nature of disorganized attachment. They emphasize the value of patience, understanding, and tailored interventions in assisting individuals on their path to healing and secure attachments.

DISORGANIZED ATTACHMENT AND RELATIONSHIPS

THE SEARCH FOR CONNECTION

*T*he desire for connection is inherent in every human being. We long to belong, to be understood, to be safe in the arms of another. For those with disorganized attachment, the search for connection is complicated by their early life experiences. The very people who were supposed to provide comfort and understanding may have caused confusion, fear, or inconsistency.

As a result, the natural desire to connect becomes entwined with fears, doubts, and conflicting emotions. It's like attempting to find a safe harbor in a stormy sea, where the lighthouse that should guide you can sometimes be the cause of the storm.

While they crave connection and intimacy, they also have fears, anxieties, and reservations about it. This creates a dichotomy in which the desire for closeness competes with the desire to protect oneself from potential harm.

Relationships aren't just about love or companionship for them; they're about trying to find consistency, understanding, and validation, and rewriting the narrative of their early attachment experiences. In essence, the search for connection transforms into a quest for healing, understanding, and reclaiming one's sense of worth and security.

PUSH-PULL DYNAMICS

The push-pull dynamic is a defining feature of disorganized attachment in relationships. It's a dance of approach and avoidance, with intense closeness followed by distancing or withdrawal. This dynamic is a result of their early experiences. They learned to seek and resist intimacy as they were drawn to their caregiver for comfort but repelled due to unpredictability or distress.

This translates into moments of deep connection and vulnerability in adult relationships, where they allow themselves to be seen and known. This closeness, however, can elicit fears or memories of past hurts, leading to withdrawal or distancing. This can be perplexing and upsetting for their partners. They feel warmth, openness, and a depth of connection, only to be met with coldness, distance, or aloofness.

It's critical to understand that this isn't about being impulsive or indecisive. It's a deeply ingrained protective mechanism, a way to navigate the turbulent waters of intimacy while avoiding potential pain.

Understanding and navigating this dynamic necessitates patience, empathy, and open communication, as well as acknowledging it as a reflection of past wounds rather than a comment on the current relationship.

FEAR OF ABANDONMENT AND BEING OVERWHELMED

Another intricate facet of disorganized attachment in relationships is the simultaneous fear of abandonment and being overwhelmed.

On one hand, there's the nagging worry that they'll be left, rejected, or deemed unworthy. This fear, rooted in early experiences of inconsistency or unpredictability, can manifest in clinginess, constant reassurance-seeking, or hypersensitivity to perceived slights.

On the other hand, there's the fear of being overwhelmed or engulfed by intimacy. Moments of deep connection, while desired, can also be daunting, triggering fears of losing one's identity or being consumed by the relationship.

This dichotomy can be difficult for both the individual and their partner. It's like walking a tightrope, where leaning too far to either side can cause anxiety and fear.

The first step is to recognize and validate these fears. Only by acknowledging them can they be addressed, thereby contributing to developing a relationship dynamic that provides both security and autonomy.

INTIMACY CHALLENGES

For those with disorganized attachment, intimacy, a cornerstone of deep and fulfilling relationships, can be a difficult terrain. While they long for the depth and closeness that intimacy provides, they must also deal with the vulnerabilities that it exposes. Opening up, letting someone in, and truly being seen can bring up old traumas, uncertainties, and self-doubts.

Sexual intimacy, in particular, can be a difficult subject. It's a vulnerable space, and past traumas or fears may surface, making it difficult to connect deeply. Moreover, emotional intimacy, in which one shares their deepest feelings, fears, and dreams, can be intimidating. While deeply connective, baring one's soul can also be a trigger, reminding them of past hurts or rejections.

Understanding this dance of desire and hesitation is critical for their partners. It's not a lack of interest or commitment; rather, it's the delicate dance of seeking closeness while protecting one's vulnerabilities.

Building intimacy requires patience, understanding, and creating a safe space where both partners can gradually open up, connect, and heal.

THE ROLE OF EXPECTATIONS

Expectations are important in shaping relationships because they influence how one perceives and interacts with their partner. These expectations are deeply colored by early experiences for those with disorganized attachment. They may expect unpredictability if they have previously experienced inconsistency. If they've been rejected before, they may be expecting it in their adult relationships.

They may have heightened expectations at times, hoping for their partner to fill the gaps left by their early caregivers. They may seek constant reassurance, validation, or understanding, hoping to find what they missed as children in adulthood.

In other cases, they may have reduced their expectations, bracing themselves for disappointment. They may not expect their partner to be there for them, as they are always expecting the other shoe to drop. These unspoken expectations shape their relationship dynamics. They impact their reactions, perceptions, and interactions, and can sometimes become self-fulfilling prophecies.

The first step toward changing these expectations is becoming aware of them. They can be rebalanced by understanding their origins and recognizing their influence, resulting in healthier and more fulfilling relationships.

COMMUNICATION BARRIERS

In the context of disorganized attachment, communication, a foundational pillar of relationships, can become fraught with difficulties. Individuals' early experiences, which may have been marked by unpredictability, confusion, or distress, may not have provided them with the tools or language to effectively express their emotions, needs, or boundaries.

They may struggle with open and direct communication because they fear rejection, misunderstanding, or conflict. This can result in avoidance, suppression, or indirect expression patterns. They may become overwhelmed by their emotions at times, making it difficult to articulate their feelings or needs coherently. Stress or conflict can reactivate old traumas, making communication even more difficult.

This can be perplexing for their partners, who may interpret the other's communication style as evasion, indifference, or inconsistency. Building effective communication skills takes time and practice. It is about creating a safe space where both partners can express themselves and be heard, understanding the underlying fears and traumas, and gradually developing a language of connection and understanding.

TRUST AND BETRAYAL

Trust, the bedrock of any relationship, is intricately woven with the fabric of attachment. For those with disorganized attachment, trust can be a fragile and complex entity. Their early experiences, where those meant to protect might have caused confusion or hurt, can make trust a daunting proposition. They might be hyper-vigilant, always on the lookout for signs of betrayal or inconsistency.

Even small actions or words, which might seem innocuous to others, can be perceived as breaches of trust, triggering intense emotional responses. On the flip side, there's also the fear of betraying oneself. In their quest for connection, they might compromise their boundaries, needs, or values, leading to feelings of self-betrayal.

Building and maintaining trust requires acknowledging these fears and wounds. It's a journey of understanding, healing, and rebuilding, where both partners work together to create a foundation of consistency, understanding, and respect.

THE CYCLE OF HOPE AND DESPAIR

For those with disorganized attachment, relationships are frequently marked by cycles of hope and despair. Deep connection and understanding, accompanied by hope and optimism, can be followed by periods of doubt, confusion, and despair.

This cycle mirrored their early experiences, in which they

experienced moments of connection with their caregiver inter-spersed with moments of unpredictability or distress. They may oscillate between these emotional states in adult relation-ships, influenced by their interactions, perceptions, and internal narratives.

Understanding this cycle is critical for the individual as well as their partner. Recognizing its roots in previous experiences can help contextualize and navigate these emotional ebbs and flows, ensuring they do not overshadow the core of the rela-tionship.

CHOOSING PARTNERS: PATTERNS TO RECOGNIZE

Our choices of partners frequently reflect our inner world, our beliefs, fears, and desires. These choices can sometimes mirror early attachment experiences for those with disorganized attachment.

They may be drawn to partners who, consciously or uncon-sciously, mirror their early caregivers' unpredictability, incon-sistency, or other characteristics. This could be a subconscious attempt to rewrite their childhood narrative in order to achieve a different outcome as an adult. However, if these patterns go unnoticed, they can lead to relationships that are characterized by confusion, pain, or the repetition of past traumas.

Awareness is the key. They can make conscious choices by understanding and recognizing these patterns, seeking partners who offer consistency, understanding, and security, thereby breaking the cycle of past traumas.

BREAKING THE CYCLE: STORIES OF HOPE

Personal transformation journeys frequently emerge from the crucible of adversity. Stories of change, growth, and newfound understanding provide inspiration and serve as a testament to the indomitable human spirit for those battling the complexities of disorganized attachment.

Emma's Odyssey

Growing up in a turbulent environment, Emma frequently felt adrift, struggling to find an anchor in the turbulent seas of relationships. Her early romantic encounters were marked by an unsettling dance of desperately clinging and then fearfully pushing away. The turning point, however, occurred when she met a therapist who introduced her to the world of attachment theories.

Emma has been able to identify her triggering moments and navigate them with increasing grace over the years, thanks to her dedication and resilience. She now lives with a partner who understands her journey, and they've built a relationship on trust, open communication, and mutual respect.

John's Path to Healing

As a child, John was always aware of a cloud of unpredictability looming over his family. This resulted in an adult life in which the fear of abandonment haunted him, making every minor conflict feel like a prelude to an unavoidable end.

However, a chance meeting at a workshop revealed the source of his fears. John set out on a journey of self-discovery, armed with this newfound knowledge. He's learned to articulate his feelings and needs with the help of group therapy and his partner's unwavering support, transforming their relationship into a haven of security and understanding.

THE BRAIN AND DISORGANIZED ATTACHMENT

NEUROSCIENCE BASICS

At its core, neuroscience investigates the intricate workings of our brain and nervous system. This vast network of neurons and synapses functions as a sophisticated command and control center, dictating our thoughts, emotions, and behaviors.

This neurological maze processes every experience we have, from the gentle caress of a loved one to the distressing sting of rejection. This processing shapes not only our immediate reactions, but also our future responses.

The brain is not a static organ with predefined functions. It is dynamic, changing as a result of our experiences, environment, and interactions. Our ability to adapt ensures our survival, growth, and development.

Our early life experiences, particularly those with our primary caregivers, play a critical role in shaping the architecture of our brain. These interactions, whether nurturing or neglectful, result in the formation of neural pathways that influence our attachment styles, emotional responses, and relational dynamics.

To truly understand disorganized attachment, it is necessary to investigate its neurological underpinnings. By doing so, we gain insights into its origins, manifestations, and healing and change possibilities.

ATTACHMENT AND BRAIN DEVELOPMENT

Our brain is a hub of activity from the moment we are born, evolving and adapting to our surroundings. Our attachment to primary caregivers is one of the most important aspects of this developmental stage.

Attachment experiences, particularly during the early formative years, have a significant impact on brain development. Interactions with caregivers that are secure and consistent foster neural pathways associated with safety, trust, and emotional regulation.

Unpredictable or distressing interactions, which are common in disorganized attachment scenarios, on the other hand, can result in the development of neural pathways associated with uncertainty, fear, and emotional dysregulation.

The areas of the brain responsible for emotional regulation, social interactions, and stress response, such as the amygdala, hippocampus, and prefrontal cortex, are particularly influenced by these early attachment experiences.

Essentially, attachment styles are more than just psychological constructs; they have physical manifestations in the brain that shape our perceptions, reactions, and relationships.

STRESS, TRAUMA, AND THE BRAIN

Stress and trauma, particularly during childhood, can have serious consequences for the brain. Prolonged exposure to distressing situations, which is typical of disorganized attachment scenarios, can lead to overactivity in the brain's stress response systems.

When children are exposed to unpredictable or traumatic situations on a regular basis, their amygdala, which is responsible for detecting threats and activating the fight-or-flight response, can become hyperactive. This state of alertness can last for a long time, making them more reactive to perceived threats, even in benign situations.

Conversely, areas such as the hippocampus, which is important for memory and emotional regulation, can be negatively impacted. Chronic stress may impair its functioning, making it difficult to process emotions or recall memories accurately.

Furthermore, the prefrontal cortex, the brain's executive center responsible for decision-making, impulse control, and emotional regulation, can be affected. This could make it difficult to make decisions, control impulses, or regulate emotions.

Distressing and unpredictable experiences associated with disorganized attachment, in essence, can reshape the brain, influencing its stress response, emotional processing, and overall functioning.

MEMORY AND RECALL

Our memories are more than just passive repositories of past events; they actively shape our perceptions, reactions, and anticipations.

Memories, particularly those from early childhood, can be fragmented or distorted in people with disorganized attachment. The unpredictability and distress they experienced may have made it difficult for them to form coherent narratives of their past.

Chronic stress or trauma can have an effect on the hippocampus, which is important for memory formation and recall. This may cause difficulty recalling specific events or, in some cases, recalling them with heightened emotionality.

Furthermore, even if these memories are not actively recalled, they can have an impact on the present. Triggers in their environment can elicit memories of past traumas, resulting in intense emotional reactions that appear disproportionate to the current situation.

It's also critical to understand that memory isn't fixed. It changes as a result of current experiences, perceptions, and narratives. Memory's dynamic nature allows for healing by allowing for the reprocessing and reframing of past traumas.

EMOTIONAL REGULATION CHALLENGES

Emotional regulation, or the ability to understand, process, and modulate our emotions, is critical to our overall well-being and relationship health. This can be a difficult domain for those with disorganized attachment.

Their early experiences, which were marked by unpredictability and distress, may not have provided them with the tools or environment in which to learn effective emotional regulation. They may have instead learned to suppress, deny, or become overwhelmed by their emotions.

The amygdala, also known as the brain's emotional center, and the prefrontal cortex, which is in charge of emotional control and modulation, both play critical roles in this process. The interplay between these areas can be disrupted in disorganized attachment scenarios, leading to increased emotional reactivity or difficulties with emotion modulation.

For many, this manifests as intense emotional responses to triggers, difficulties in understanding or expressing their emotions, or a pervasive sense of emotional confusion or turmoil. However, with understanding, support, and therapeutic interventions, these challenges can be addressed, paving the way for better emotional understanding and regulation.

NEURAL PATHWAYS AND CHANGE

Every experience, thought, or emotion we have creates or reinforces neural pathways in our brains. These pathways, like wellworn forest paths, govern our automatic reactions, behaviors, and patterns.

Specific neural pathways are formed as a result of disorganized attachment experiences and their associated thoughts, emotions, and reactions. These pathways can become our default over time, influencing our perceptions, reactions, and relationships.

The brain, on the other hand, is not static. It is dynamic, evolving, and adapting all the time. Neuroplasticity, or the ability to change, provides hope. New experiences can create or strengthen new pathways, just as certain experiences created or reinforced specific pathways.

Positive experiences, therapeutic interventions, and conscious efforts can all aid in rewiring the brain, creating pathways associated with security, trust, and emotional regulation. While difficult, this process emphasizes the possibility of change, healing, and growth.

THE PLASTICITY OF THE BRAIN

The brain's plasticity is one of neuroscience's most profound discoveries. Research shows that our brains can change, adapt, and evolve throughout our lives, contrary to previous beliefs that the brain is static after childhood.

This plasticity extends beyond the formation of new neural connections. It includes the strengthening of existing connections, the weakening or pruning of redundant or ineffective connections, and the generation of new neurons in specific brain regions.

This plasticity gives hope to those who have disorganized attachment. Their early experiences, while influential, do not foretell their future. Their brains can adapt with the right interventions, support, and experiences, paving the way for healing, growth, and change.

This brain's transformative ability highlights the human spirit's resilience, emphasizing that change, healing, and growth are always possible.

BRAIN-BASED STRATEGIES FOR HEALING

Understanding the neurological foundations of disorganized attachment provides more than just insights; it also provides concrete strategies for healing and change. These neuroscience-based strategies aim to reshape the brain's architecture while also facilitating healing and growth.

For example, Cognitive Behavioral Therapy (CBT) focuses on identifying and challenging unhelpful thoughts, beliefs, and behaviors. This aids in forming new neural pathways associated with healthier thought and behavior patterns.

Another therapeutic intervention is Eye Movement Desensitization and Reprocessing (EMDR), which is specifically designed to aid in the processing and reprocessing of traumatic memories, facilitating their integration and reducing their emotional charge.

Mindfulness and meditation, by encouraging present-moment awareness and emotional regulation, assist in modulating amygdala activity and strengthening the prefrontal cortex. (See next section.)

Individuals can embark on a healing journey by incorporating these and other brain-based strategies, utilizing the brain's plasticity to effect long-term change.

MEDITATION AND MINDFULNESS

Meditation and mindfulness stand out among brain-based healing strategies for their ease of use, accessibility, and profound effects. These practices, rooted in ancient traditions, now have solid support from modern neuroscience.

Meditation can increase gray matter density in areas associated with emotional regulation, memory, and self-awareness by encouraging focused attention and awareness. It aids in modulating amygdala activity, lowering reactivity to perceived threats.

Mindfulness, the practice of being present and nonjudgmentally aware, provides tools for navigating the emotional turmoil frequently associated with disorganized attachment. It allows individuals to process emotions without becoming overwhelmed by cultivating a compassionate, observing stance.

Regular meditation and mindfulness practice can result in tangible neurological changes, highlighting their potential to facilitate healing, growth, and change for those dealing with disorganized attachment.

REAL-LIFE TRANSFORMATIONS: BRAIN TRAINING STORIES

Behind every scientific principle or breakthrough is a tapestry of human stories rich in emotion, trials, and revelations. Through the experiences of those who have bravely walked this path, the journey to understanding and healing disorganized attachment through the lens of neuroscience becomes vivid and relatable.

Sarah's Neurofeedback Odyssey

Sarah's life was marked by bouts of intense anxiety and erratic emotional shifts. She struggled for years to find the right therapeutic approach to address the root of her problems. Then she learned about neurofeedback. Sarah felt a mixture of apprehension and hope as electrodes were placed on her scalp to measure her brain's electrical activity.

This real-time feedback provided insights into her brain's

functioning after several sessions. Sarah learned to influence her brain waves with the help of skilled practitioners, eventually discovering a sense of calm and regulation she had never felt before. She now attributes neurofeedback to not only improving her emotional stability but also her cognitive functions, resulting in a richer, more balanced life.

James' Mindfulness Awakening

On the outside, James seemed to have it all – a successful career, a loving family, and a bustling social life. Internally, however, he struggled with bouts of disassociation, a legacy of his traumatic childhood. A colleague introduced him to the world of mindfulness, which at first felt foreign and intimidating to James.

With persistence, he began to embrace the moments of silence, focusing on his breath and grounding himself in the present. The chaotic whirlwind of emotions began to settle over time. The storms that had threatened to capsize him had become manageable waves. Within himself, James discovered a sanctuary of clarity and serenity. This newfound inner peace radiated outward, profoundly influencing his interactions and relationships.

Sarah's, James', and others' journeys are powerful testaments to the synergies between cutting-edge neuroscience and personal resilience. Each story captures the essence of transformation, offering both hope and a road map for those attempting to navigate the complicated landscape of disorganized attachment. We see the remarkable adaptability of the human brain and its limitless potential for healing and growth through their stories.

PSYCHOLOGICAL PERSPECTIVES

PSYCHODYNAMIC VIEWS

*T*he psychodynamic approach provides profound insights into disorganized attachment by delving into the realm of the unconscious. It investigates the deep-seated memories, desires, and fears that shape behavior, based on Freud's theories and further developed by later psycho-analysts.

Early childhood experiences, particularly relationships with primary caregivers, have a significant influence on this view-point. These formative years' unresolved conflicts, internalized feelings, and unconscious desires can influence adult relation-ships, behaviors, and self-concept.

Transference, or the projection of past emotions onto current relationships, is a common theme in psychodynamic therapy. This could manifest as a person with disorganized attachment projecting feelings associated with inconsistent caregivers onto current partners or therapists.

Countertransference, in which therapists project their unresolved feelings onto clients, is also an important factor to consider. Therapists must be acutely aware of this dynamic in order to keep the therapy client-centered.

In psychodynamic therapy, the therapeutic space is one of exploration, reflection, and insight. Clients can unearth, understand, and integrate these unconscious influences through free association, dream analysis, and resistance explorations.

Basically, the psychodynamic viewpoint provides a deep dive into the unconscious mind, illuminating the hidden influences of disorganized attachment and paving the way for healing through comprehension.

COGNITIVE-BEHAVIORAL INSIGHTS

Cognitive Behavioral Therapy (CBT) is based on the premise that our thoughts, emotions, and behaviors are all inextricably linked. It is possible to facilitate behavioral and emotional change by identifying and challenging maladaptive thoughts and beliefs.

Certain core beliefs about self-worth, trust, or relationships may be deeply ingrained in someone with disorganized attachment. These beliefs, which are frequently based on early experiences, can have an impact on current perceptions, emotions, and reactions.

CBT provides tools for identifying these beliefs, understanding their origins, and questioning their validity. Individuals can develop healthier, more adaptive beliefs through thought records, behavioral experiments, and cognitive restructuring.

CBT emphasizes not only introspection but also active behavior change. To facilitate this change, exposure exercises, role-playing, and behavioral activation are commonly used strategies.

It's a team effort, with the therapist and client working together to set goals, identify challenges, and devise solutions.

CBT, because of its structured, goal-oriented nature, provides concrete tools and techniques for those dealing with disorganized attachment, facilitating insight and fostering change.

HUMANISTIC AND PERSON-CENTERED APPROACHES

The humanistic and person-centered approach, which is based on Carl Rogers' work, believes in people's inherent goodness and growth potential. It believes that, given the right circumstances, every individual is capable of self-awareness, change, and growth.

The therapist's role in this approach is not that of an expert but rather that of a facilitator. They provide an environment that fosters empathy, unconditional positive regard, and congruence, allowing clients to explore, understand, and integrate their feelings and experiences.

This approach provides a corrective relational experience for those who have disorganized attachment. The therapist's consistent, empathetic, and non-judgmental stance can compensate for the unpredictability and inconsistency they may have experienced in early relationships.

Individuals are empowered to make choices that are aligned with their true selves when self-awareness and self-acceptance are fostered, facilitating growth and change.

The emphasis is on the present moment and the client's subjective experience, allowing for genuine self-exploration and self-expression.

The humanistic and person-centered approach provides a compassionate, empathetic space for healing founded on the transformative power of genuine human connection.

EXISTENTIALIST PERSPECTIVES

Existential therapy delves into the fundamental questions of life, exploring themes such as freedom, responsibility, meaning, and isolation. It addresses the inherent anxieties associated with existence, drawing on the philosophies of existential thinkers such as Sartre, Kierkegaard, and Nietzsche.

Existential therapy provides a forum for those with disorganized attachment to explore feelings of isolation, alienation, or meaninglessness that may have arisen from their early relational experiences.

It emphasizes personal freedom and responsibility, emphasizing that individuals, regardless of their past experiences, have the agency to make choices and create meaning in their lives.

In existential therapy, the therapeutic space is one of deep reflection, introspection, and philosophical exploration. It is not just about treating symptoms but also about addressing the underlying existential dilemmas.

By fostering a genuine confrontation with these existential

concerns, individuals can find clarity, purpose, and a renewed sense of meaning, paving the way for authentic existence.

Existential therapy provides a profound exploration of life's inherent challenges and quandaries, guiding individuals toward authentic, meaningful existence.

THE ROLE OF NARRATIVE THERAPY

Narrative therapy is based on the idea that the narratives or stories we tell ourselves shape our identities. These narratives, which are influenced by societal norms, cultural expectations, and personal experiences, have the potential to empower or constrain us.

Someone with disorganized attachment may have a narrative of unworthiness, distrust, or chaos. These early experience-based stories can shape their adult perceptions, emotions, and behaviors.

Narrative therapy's role is to assist individuals in identifying these dominant narratives, understanding their origins, and, most importantly, re-authoring them. Individuals can view these narratives as separate from their identity by externalizing the problem, allowing for critical reflection and re-evaluation.

Individuals can create alternative narratives that are more closely aligned with their desired identity and values by using techniques such as re-authoring, re-membering, and scaffolding.

Individuals who transform their narratives change not only their self-perception but also their interactions with the world, facilitating healing, growth, and change.

FAMILY SYSTEMS AND ATTACHMENT

Attachment patterns do not exist in a vacuum; they are deeply ingrained in family dynamics. The family systems theory, pioneered by therapists like Murray Bowen and Virginia Satir, sees the family as an interconnected unit whose dynamics influence individual behaviors and emotions.

Understanding these dynamics can provide profound insights for those who have disorganized attachment. The unpredictability or inconsistency they experienced could have been a symptom of a larger family pattern influenced by generational traumas, parental dynamics, or external stressors.

With its systemic lens, family therapy provides a platform for exploring and addressing these patterns. It creates an environment conducive to collective healing and change by encouraging communication, understanding, and empathy among family members.

Some of the topics covered in family therapy include family roles, communication patterns, and boundary dynamics. Families can break the cycle of dysfunctional attachment by understanding and addressing these issues, paving the way for healthier relationships.

The family systems perspective, fundamentally, emphasizes the interconnectedness of attachment patterns, emphasizing the role of collective healing in addressing disorganized attachment.

THE THERAPEUTIC RELATIONSHIP

The relationship between the therapist and the client is at the heart of every therapeutic intervention. This trusting, empathic, and understanding relationship serves as a crucible for healing, change, and growth.

The therapeutic relationship is especially important for people who have disorganized attachment. It provides a corrective relational experience, a counterpoint to the inconsistency and unpredictability they may have encountered in previous relationships.

The therapist's role is multifaceted. They provide empathy, understanding, and insight while also challenging, provoking, and guiding. They create an environment conducive to introspection, reflection, and change by maintaining this delicate balance.

The therapeutic alliance, or the bond of trust and collaboration that exists between the therapist and the client, is critical. Research consistently highlights its importance in therapeutic outcomes, emphasizing its role as a key change agent.

The therapeutic relationship embodies the transformative power of genuine human connection, serving as a beacon of hope, understanding, and change for those struggling with disorganized attachment.

THE POWER OF INSIGHT

The key to transformation is insight, or a deep understanding of oneself and one's patterns. Insight opens the door to conscious choice, change, and growth by illuminating the underlying beliefs, feelings, and behaviors.

Insight can be both challenging and liberating for someone with disorganized attachment. It entails confronting painful memories, understanding their significance, and acknowledging their influence on current behavior and emotions.

However, understanding comes with empowerment. Individuals can free themselves from the unconscious influences of the past by recognizing these patterns.

The therapeutic environment, with its emphasis on introspection, reflection, and comprehension, fosters this insight. Therapists guide clients to a deeper understanding of themselves through explorations, challenges, and discussions.

Insight is a portal to change, providing clarity, understanding, and empowerment to those navigating the turbulent waters of disorganized attachment.

THE ROLE OF RESILIENCE

Resilience, or the ability to recover from adversity, is especially important in the journey of healing from disorganized attachment. Despite past challenges and traumas, the capacity for growth, change, and renewal remains.

Resilience may manifest in those with disorganized attachment as the ability to form meaningful relationships despite early experiences or the ability to find hope, meaning, and purpose despite challenges.

Recognizing and harnessing one's strengths, seeking support, and cultivating a growth mindset all contribute to resilience. Individuals can navigate life's adversities with grace, grit, and determination if they view challenges as opportunities for growth and recognize their inherent capacity for change.

The therapeutic environment, with its emphasis on empowerment, strength, and growth, fosters this resilience. Therapists guide clients toward recognizing and harnessing their resilience by exploring past successes, strengths, and resources.

Resilience serves as a guiding light, demonstrating the

indomitable human spirit's ability to heal, grow, and thrive in the face of adversity.

INTEGRATIVE APPROACHES TO HEALING

No single approach to psychology has all of the answers. Recognizing this, integrative therapy seeks to integrate elements from various therapeutic modalities, resulting in a personalized, holistic approach to healing.

This may entail combining insights from psychodynamic therapy, CBT strategies, and the empathetic stance of human-istic therapy for someone with disorganized attachment. Therapy can thus address both deep-seated unconscious influences and current challenges.

Integrative therapy focuses on the individual's unique needs, challenges, and goals. It provides a holistic, comprehensive approach to healing by combining the strengths of various therapeutic modalities.

Integrative therapy acknowledges the multifaceted nature of human experience by providing a comprehensive, tailored approach to healing, growth, and change.

BODY-CENTERED APPROACHES

THE MIND-BODY CONNECTION

*F*or centuries, various cultures have recognized the intricate link between the mind and body. Modern science, too, emphasizes the two-way communication that exists between our physical selves and our emotional and psychological states.

This connection is especially poignant for people with disorganized attachment. Early childhood emotional traumas and inconsistencies frequently manifest as physical tensions, pains, or somatic symptoms.

Understanding this link is essential for holistic healing. Addressing only the cognitive or emotional aspects of trauma is insufficient; one must also address its physical imprints.

Emerging research in psychoneuroimmunology investigates how emotional states affect immune function, stress response, and overall health. This emphasizes the significance of a holistic approach to healing.

In effect, the mind-body connection emphasizes the interplay between our physical and emotional selves, emphasizing the importance of holistic interventions that address both domains in the healing journey.

TRAUMA AND THE BODY

Trauma leaves indelible marks on our bodies as well as our minds. While essential for survival, the "fight, flight, or freeze" response can become dysregulated in the face of chronic or severe trauma.

The unpredictability and inconsistency of early relationships may have repeatedly activated this stress response in those with disorganized attachment. This can lead to a variety of physical issues, such as chronic tension, digestive issues, or an increased state of alertness.

The body, in its wisdom, often stores traumatic memories or emotions. These might manifest as tension in specific areas, such as a tightened jaw, hunched shoulders, or constricted breathing.

Recognizing and addressing these physical manifestations is crucial for holistic healing. By releasing these stored tensions and recalibrating the body's stress response, one can pave the way for deeper emotional and psychological healing.

Basically, the body functions as both a repository and a portal. Understanding and addressing the physical imprints of trauma can open the door to deeper layers of healing and integration.

BREATHWORK FOR HEALING

The breath, which is frequently overlooked, acts as a powerful link between the conscious and unconscious, the body and the mind. Breathwork, a collection of techniques that involve conscious breathing regulation, has the potential to be transformative for healing.

Breathwork can be a grounding and regulating practice for those who have disorganized attachment. Individuals can activate the parasympathetic nervous system, promoting relaxation and calm, by focusing on the rhythm, depth, and pattern of their breathing.

Various techniques, ranging from pranayama's deep belly breathing to the transformative patterns of holotropic breathwork, provide avenues for exploration and healing. Each has its advantages, ranging from immediate stress relief to profound emotional release.

Breathing exercises can also help individuals recognize and regulate their emotional and physiological responses to stress or triggers.

The breath provides a platform for mindfulness, grounding, and self-regulation by acting as an anchor to the present moment, making it an invaluable tool in the healing arsenal.

Breathwork illuminates the transformative power of the breath by providing techniques for relaxation, grounding, and profound emotional healing.

SOMATIC EXPERIENCING

Somatic Experiencing (SE), developed by Dr. Peter Levine, is a body-centered approach designed specifically to address trauma. It is based on the idea that trauma disrupts the body's natural equilibrium, and that restoring this balance can help with healing.

SE provides a platform for individuals with disorganized attachment to explore and release the physical manifestations of early traumas. They can access stored emotions or memories by tuning into bodily sensations, movements, or impulses.

The SE therapist serves as a guide, assisting clients in navigating these feelings, offering support, and ensuring that the process is safe and contained.

The goal is to process and integrate traumatic events, allowing the body to complete its natural stress response and return to a state of equilibrium.

SE provides a profound avenue for trauma resolution by focusing on the "felt sense" and the innate wisdom of the body, facilitating healing, integration, and wholeness.

Somatic Experiencing emphasizes the body's innate healing capacity, providing a gentle, embodied approach to trauma resolution.

YOGA AND ATTACHMENT

Yoga, an ancient Indian philosophy-based practice, is more than just a form of physical exercise; it is a holistic system that integrates the mind, body, and spirit. Its emphasis on mindfulness, breath, and bodily awareness makes it especially effective for those dealing with the difficulties of disorganized attachment.

Yoga asanas, or physical postures, provide a platform for exploring and releasing bodily tensions. These postures can serve as a gateway to stored emotions or memories for someone with disorganized attachment, facilitating release and integration.

Pranayama, or breathwork in yoga, enhances this process by encouraging relaxation, grounding, and self-awareness.

Yoga's philosophical tenets, which emphasize non-attachment, compassion, and present-moment awareness, provide valuable insights and guidance for those on the healing path.

Yoga provides a holistic platform for healing, integration, and growth by fostering a deep sense of connection to oneself, others, and the universe at large.

Yoga, in essence, illuminates the path to wholeness by integrating the physical, emotional, and spiritual dimensions of the self, allowing for profound healing and transformation.

DANCE AND MOVEMENT THERAPIES

For millennia, dance has been used as a form of expression, celebration, and healing across cultures. This power is harnessed by dance and movement therapies, which use movement as a medium for exploration, expression, and healing.

These therapies provide a nonverbal platform for those with disorganized attachment to explore and express emotions. The rhythmic, fluid movements can be used to counteract the rigidity or tension caused by trauma.

Clients can explore patterns of movement, postures, or gestures that resonate with their emotional state with the help of a trained therapist, facilitating expression, release, and integration.

Dance therapy group settings can also foster connection, empathy, and mutual support, providing a corrective relational experience for those with challenging attachment histories.

Basically, dance and movement therapies highlight movement's therapeutic power by providing a dynamic, embodied platform for exploration, expression, and healing.

TOUCH AND HEALING

Touch, a basic human need, is essential for bonding, comfort, and healing. Touch, on the other hand, may be fraught with ambiguity for those with disorganized attachment, triggering memories of inconsistency or even trauma.

When used wisely and ethically in therapeutic settings, touch can be a powerful tool for healing. Comfort, grounding, and connection can be provided by techniques such as craniosacral therapy, therapeutic massage, or even simple handholding.

Those who have experienced touch-related trauma or inconsistency may begin their journey by establishing boundaries, rebuilding trust, and gradually reintroducing touch in safe, contained ways.

The goal is to rebalance the body's reaction to touch, transforming it from a potential trigger to a source of comfort, connection, and healing.

Therapeutic touch emphasizes the healing potential of human connection, providing comfort, grounding, and support to those on the healing journey.

GROUNDING TECHNIQUES

Grounding techniques, as the name implies, are tools that assist people in anchoring themselves to the present moment. These techniques are invaluable for those with disorganized attachment, who may frequently feel overwhelmed or dissociated as a result of past traumas.

Simple practices such as focusing on one's breath, feeling one's feet on the ground, or grasping a tactile object can help one step back from overwhelming emotions or memories.

More advanced techniques may include visualization, in which people imagine themselves rooted to the earth and drawing strength and stability from its core.

Grounding techniques not only provide immediate relief in times of stress, but they also foster a deeper sense of connection to oneself and one's surroundings.

Individuals can improve their resilience by regularly practicing these techniques, allowing them to navigate triggers, stressors, or emotional upheavals with grace and equanimity.

Grounding techniques illuminate the path to stability, connection, and presence, providing invaluable tools for those navigating the difficulties of disorganized attachment.

BODY-BASED MINDFULNESS PRACTICES

Mindfulness, or the art of being fully present in the moment, has its roots in ancient Buddhist practices. However, it has gained widespread acceptance in modern therapeutic settings due to its myriad benefits. Body-based mindfulness practices focus on physical sensations, providing a grounding, exploration, and healing platform.

Practices such as the body scan, in which people tune into sensations in various parts of their bodies, promote awareness, relaxation, and release.

For those who have disorganized attachment, these practices can act as a bridge, reconnecting them to their bodies, which are frequently alienated or ignored as a result of past traumas.

Individuals can foster connection, integration, and healing by regularly tuning into bodily sensations, whether it's the rhythm of the breath, the beat of the heart, or the subtle play of emotions.

Body-based mindfulness practices highlight the transformative power of present-moment awareness by providing tools for grounding, connection, and holistic healing.

STORIES OF PHYSICAL LIBERATION

The human body is more than just a container; it is a complex map of experiences, emotions, and memories. Chronic tension, pain, and discomfort can result from the physical embodiment of our histories. However, the body has the capacity for profound healing and liberation. Sarah, Mark, and Anna's stories demonstrate the transformative journeys that people can take when they embrace body-centered approaches.

Sarah's Journey with Somatic Experiencing

Sarah used to feel like a coiled spring as a child, her muscles tense and ready to spring into action or curl up for protection. This stress carried over into adulthood, manifesting as chronic pain, migraines, and sleep disturbances.

Sarah's breakthrough occurred during a somatic-experiencing workshop. She was encouraged by a skilled therapist to deeply feel her bodily sensations without judgment. As she became more aware of these sensations, buried memories of insecurity and fear began to surface. Every session was filled with tears, laughter, and immense relief. Sarah's physical pain subsided over time, but she also felt emotionally lighter, more grounded, and connected.

Mark and the Healing Power of Yoga

With his lean physique and graceful yoga postures, Mark appeared to outsiders as the epitome of calm and balance. But many people were unaware of his harrowing journey to the mat. Mark had always struggled with erratic emotions and a pervasive sense of disconnect due to growing up in a chaotic household. Yoga was initially just another physical exercise for him. However, as he dug deeper, he recognized its therapeutic potential.

The asanas evolved into more than just poses; they expressed his internal struggles and triumphs. Pranayama (breathing exercises) and meditation became anchors for him, assisting him in navigating and integrating fragmented memories and emotions. Mark now not only enjoys inner peace but also actively promotes yoga as a healing tool for those struggling with attachment issues.

Anna's Dance of Liberation

Anna had always loved to dance. But it wasn't until she was an adult that she realized how dance could be used as a therapeutic outlet. During a particularly difficult period, she happened upon a dance therapy workshop. Initially hesitant, she soon became engrossed in the rhythm and movements.

It became a vehicle for her to express emotions that were too intense to express verbally. Years of suppressed feelings - pain, joy, anger, and love - poured out as she swayed, twirled, and leaped. Anna's sanctuary became the dance floor, a place where she felt truly free and integrated.

These authentic narratives paint a vivid picture of the myriad ways in which the body can serve as a barometer of our internal states as well as a tool for profound healing. We see glimpses of the vast possibilities for transformation and liberation inherent in body-centered approaches in Sarah's sensory exploration, Mark's disciplined yoga practice, and Anna's free-flowing dance movements. Their stories are a testament to the tenacity of the human spirit and the power of physical expression.

DAILY HABITS AND ROUTINES

THE POWER OF ROUTINE

*R*outines emerge as anchors in an unpredictable world, providing stability, predictability, and comfort. They shape our days, influence our moods, and serve as the foundation of our lives.

The presence of a routine can be especially beneficial for people dealing with disorganized attachment. It provides an antidote to the inconsistency and unpredictability of early childhood experiences, fostering a sense of security and predictability.

Creating daily habits is more than just adding structure; it is about cultivating practices that nourish the mind, body, and spirit. When chosen mindfully, each routine can be a step toward healing, growth, and self-awareness.

Routine consistency fosters resilience. As these practices

become ingrained, they serve as touchpoints of stability, assisting in navigating life's ups and downs with grace and equanimity.

Routines become self-care rituals for many people. They are pauses for reflection and nourishment that fortify them against external stressors and internal upheavals.

The power of routine is found not only in its structure but also in its capacity for healing, growth, and transformation.

MORNING RITUALS FOR GROUNDING

The way we start our days often sets the tone for the rest of the day. Morning rituals, as a result, have enormous potential, providing a platform for grounding, intention-setting, and self-care.

Many people start their days with mindfulness practices like meditation or deep breathing. These quiet moments allow them to reconnect with themselves and set an intention for the day ahead.

Others may prefer physical activities such as yoga or a morning walk. The act of moving, especially when coordinated with the breath, provides grounding and awakens the body and mind.

Another enriching morning ritual is reading, even if only for a few minutes. A spiritual text, a motivational book, or even a daily journal provides food for thought, shaping one's perspective for the day.

Affirmations in the morning, a powerful tool for cognitive restructuring, can help instill positivity, confidence, and clarity. These affirmations, when repeated daily, can help to reset one's self-beliefs and worldview.

The simple act of sipping a warm beverage in silence while watching the world awaken becomes a ritual of presence, gratitude, and connection for some.

Morning rituals serve as the foundation of the day, providing grounding, nourishment, and direction.

NUTRITION AND MENTAL HEALTH

When viewed through the lens of mental health, the adage "You are what you eat" takes on new meaning. Nutrition, which is frequently overlooked, plays an important role in emotional and psychological well-being.

Certain foods, high in antioxidants, omega-3 fatty acids, and vitamins, have been shown to improve brain health, potentially alleviating depression, anxiety, and cognitive decline symptoms.

Paying attention to nutrition becomes even more important for those with disorganized attachment. The physical and emotional stresses caused by early traumas can tax the body, making nutrition a top priority.

Furthermore, the act of eating can be therapeutic in and of itself. Mindful eating, in which each bite is savored with presence and gratitude, can be a grounding and enriching experience.

Avoiding excessive caffeine, refined sugars, and processed foods while increasing your intake of whole grains, lean proteins, fruits, and vegetables can have a significant impact on your mood, energy levels, and overall well-being.

Nutrition is more than just what we eat; it is also about how we eat. Sharing meals with loved ones, cooking with intention and love, and expressing gratitude for the nourishment provided all contribute to the act of eating.

Nutrition emphasizes the intricate relationship between physical nourishment and mental health, emphasizing the importance of mindful, balanced eating in overall well-being.

SLEEP HYGIENE FOR EMOTIONAL REGULATION

Sleep, a basic human requirement, has enormous power in regulating our emotions, cognitive functions, and overall health. Inadequate or disrupted sleep can exacerbate mental health issues by lowering resilience and amplifying emotional reactivity.

Sleep may be difficult for people who have a disorganized attachment. Memories, anxieties, or physical discomforts may disrupt the sleep cycle, resulting in a cascade of emotional and cognitive difficulties.

Establishing good sleeping habits becomes critical. Maintaining a consistent sleep schedule, creating a conducive sleep environment with dim lighting and comfortable bedding, and avoiding stimulants such as caffeine or screen time before bedtime are all part of this.

Deep breathing, progressive muscle relaxation, and guided visualizations are all relaxation techniques that can help with the transition into sleep and reduce nighttime anxiety.

The quality of sleep is just as important as the quantity. Getting enough deep, restorative sleep can improve cognitive functions, emotional regulation, and overall vitality.

Understanding the relationship between sleep and emotional well-being can inspire proactive measures to make sleep a restorative, healing experience.

Sleep hygiene practices emphasize the importance of restful, consistent sleep in emotional regulation, cognitive function, and overall mental health.

PHYSICAL ACTIVITY AND MENTAL WELLBEING

Physical activity, frequently lauded for its role in physical health, also plays an important role in mental health. Movement has a profound effect on mood, cognition, and stress levels, whether it is a brisk walk, a yoga session, or a rigorous gym workout.

Endorphins are the body's natural mood elevators, which are released during physical activity. They alleviate depression and anxiety symptoms while instilling a sense of well-being.

Physical activity provides an outlet, a way to channel emotions, memories, or sensations that may feel overwhelming for those with disorganized attachment. Running and swimming, for example, can be meditative due to their rhythmic, repetitive nature, providing a form of moving mindfulness.

Group activities such as dance classes, team sports, and group fitness sessions promote social connection by providing camaraderie, mutual support, and a sense of belonging.

Mountain climbing, marathons, and martial arts can all turn into journeys of self-discovery, resilience building, and empowerment.

Physical activity illuminates the path to holistic well-being by emphasizing the intricate relationship between movement, mood, and mental health.

JOURNALING FOR INSIGHT AND CLARITY

The simple yet profound act of writing provides a platform for introspection, expression, and clarity. Journaling, a structured form of writing, has enormous therapeutic potential, particularly for those dealing with the difficulties of disorganized attachment.

Individuals can gain insight into patterns, triggers, or underlying beliefs by writing down thoughts, emotions, or memories. This self-awareness serves as the foundation for transformation, growth, and healing.

Journaling provides a safe, nonjudgmental environment for expression. Traumatic memories, suppressed emotions, or hidden fears can all find an outlet and be released, reducing their emotional charge.

Journaling prompts can help to guide introspection and allow for the exploration of specific themes, challenges, or goals.

Journaling can become a form of meditation for some, a moment of pause, reflection, and connection with oneself. Additionally, it emphasizes the therapeutic power of expression by providing tools for introspection, clarity, and self-understanding.

MINDFUL PRACTICES FOR DAILY LIFE

Mindfulness, the art of present-moment awareness, transcends structured practices, weaving its way into daily life. These practices, whether mindful eating, mindful walking, or simply mindful breathing, provide grounding, clarity, and connection.

The constant pull of past traumas or anxieties can be overwhelming for those with disorganized attachment. Mindful practices provide a counterbalance by bringing people back to the present moment, reducing rumination, and encouraging presence.

The simplicity of mindfulness is its beauty. It does not necessitate any particular postures, tools, or environments. It is possible to become meditative while doing dishes, driving, or simply sipping a cup of tea.

Regular mindful practices build resilience, emotional regulation, and cognitive clarity, preparing people to face life's challenges with grace and equanimity.

Daily mindful practices highlight the transformative power of present-moment awareness, providing tools for grounding, connection, and holistic well-being.

THE ROLE OF NATURE AND OUTDOORS

Nature, with its many wonders, provides comfort, inspiration, and healing. The simple act of being outside has profound effects on mental health, whether it's a walk in the park, a hike in the mountains, or a day at the beach.

Nature provides a space of consistency, predictability, and wonder for those dealing with disorganized attachment. Nature's rhythmic patterns, whether the ebb and flow of the tides, the changing seasons, or the chirping of birds, provide grounding and connection.

Nature-based therapies, such as forest bathing or eco-therapy, highlight the therapeutic potential of nature by allowing for exploration, expression, and healing.

Being in nature lowers cortisol levels, the stress hormone, and instills a sense of calm, clarity, and well-being.

The role of nature and the outdoors emphasizes the natural world's healing power, emphasizing its potential in fostering mental health, well-being, and holistic healing.

SOCIAL CONNECTION AND ITS BENEFITS

Humans, by nature social creatures, thrive on connection. Family, romantic, and platonic relationships weave the fabric of our lives, influencing our mental, emotional, and even physical health.

Social connections can be difficult but necessary for people who have disorganized attachment. While past traumas may make it difficult to trust, be intimate, or be vulnerable, the right relationships provide support, validation, and healing.

A sense of belonging, purpose, and mutual support can be fostered by being a part of a community, whether it's a support group, a hobby club, or even a religious congregation.

Positive social interactions, even if they are brief, such as a conversation with a neighbor or a kind gesture from a stranger, can lift one's mood and instill a sense of belonging.

Social connection illuminates the path to overall well-being by emphasizing the importance of relationships in fostering mental health, support, and mutual growth.

TESTIMONIALS: HABITS THAT TRANSFORMED LIVES

Daily routines and habits can lay the groundwork for long-term positive changes in one's life. Small changes can sometimes result in profound shifts in perspective, emotional states, and overall well-being. In this section, we delve deeper into the lives of Laura, Steven, Lily, and Sam. We'll look at the power of habits in shaping our mental landscapes and guiding us toward healing through their personal stories.

Laura's Morning of Mindfulness

Laura's mornings used to consist of repeatedly hitting the snooze button, followed by a mad dash out the door. The constant rush left her feeling frazzled and set the tone for the rest of her day. When she attended a mindfulness workshop, everything changed. Laura was inspired to create a morning routine centered on stillness and introspection.

She began each day with a 10-minute meditation, focusing on her breath and grounding herself in the present moment. She'd then journal, expressing her thoughts, feelings, and intentions for the day. She'd finish her ritual by listing three things she was thankful for. This practice not only centered her, but it also changed her perspective on life. Laura gradually began to approach her days with more clarity, purpose, and gratitude.

Steven's Nightly Reflections

Steven had always felt weighed down by his past. Suppressed memories and suppressed emotions left him disconnected and at times desolate. Journaling was suggested by a therapist as a way to confront and process these feelings. Steven, who was initially skeptical, soon found solace in the pages of his diary.

Every night, under the soft light of his bedside lamp, he'd jot down his thoughts, from joy to deep sorrow. This practice evolved into a sacred space for reflection, allowing him to face his fears, celebrate his accomplishments, and set future intentions. Writing provided Steven with clarity, a renewed sense of hope, and a stronger connection to his authentic self.

Lily's Nature Retreats

Lily had little contact with nature as a child growing up in a big city. She felt an innate pull towards the great outdoors after a particularly taxing period in her life. She decided to join a local hiking group on a whim. The tranquility of the woods, the chirping of birds, and the rhythmic pattern of her footsteps on the trail were all soothing.

Her weekly hikes soon expanded to include birdwatching, which not only connected her with nature but also introduced her to a thriving community of enthusiasts. She found support, camaraderie, and shared awe of the natural world with these people. Nature became Lily's refuge, a place for rest, reflection, and a deep connection.

Sam's Quest for Restful Sleep

Insomnia had plagued Sam for years. He'd wake up exhausted and irritable after a night of tossing and turning. Desperate for a change, he sought advice and came across the concept of sleep hygiene. Sam, intrigued, devised a strict pre-sleep routine.

His nights started with a warm bath, followed by a relaxing book. He then practiced progressive muscle relaxation, consciously relaxing every muscle in his body. Finally, guided visualizations would take him to tranquil landscapes, easing his transition into a deep sleep. Not only did Sam's sleep improve over time, but so did his overall well-being and mental clarity.

Laura, Steven, Lily, and Sam's journeys demonstrate the remarkable impact that daily habits can have on our well-being. These testimonials highlight the transformative power of routines, whether it's a morning of mindfulness, nightly reflections, weekly nature retreats, or a dedicated sleep routine. They are a testament to the human spirit's resilience and the numerous ways in which we can navigate challenges and promote holistic healing.

NURTURING SECURE ATTACHMENTS

UNDERSTANDING SECURE ATTACHMENT

*a*t its core, secure attachment is an emotional bond that fosters a sense of safety and closeness between individuals. This bond develops as a result of consistent, responsive care during a person's formative years. A child who has been shown consistent love and understanding grows up knowing that they are valued, creating a safe harbor for them to return to no matter what life throws at them.

It is a mistake to think of attachment as a fixed childhood outcome. Our attachment styles are shaped by the experiences we have, both positive and negative, throughout our lives. These personalities not only reflect our past but also shape our present, influencing our friendships, parent-child relationships, and even our relationship with ourselves.

The scope of secure attachment is an important aspect.

People frequently limit their understanding of it to romantic bonds. Its tendrils, however, reach into every relationship, influencing how we perceive and interact with the world. This affects how trust is established, comfort is sought, and conflict is resolved in various relationships.

Furthermore, achieving secure attachment isn't about being perfect. No relationship, no matter how strong, is without conflicts or misunderstandings. What matters is the bond's tenacity, the belief that, in the end, both parties will feel acknowledged and valued.

When one recognizes the importance of secure attachment, it serves as a compass. It directs people toward practices and behaviors that reinforce safety and understanding in relationships, resulting in a virtuous cycle.

BUILDING TRUST CONSISTENTLY

Trust is more than a feeling; it is an action. It is the bedrock upon which all else rests in the context of secure attachment. Trust is built not through grand gestures or grand pronouncements, but through small, consistent acts that demonstrate dependability.

Every relationship experiences moments of vulnerability. Consistency in actions and behavior takes center stage during such times. When one can trust their partner or friend to be there for them, especially during difficult times, it creates an environment in which both parties can feel safe and understood.

The journey to trust is more like a marathon than a sprint. It is built on shared experiences, collective memories, and jointly overcoming challenges. It's critical to think of trust as a living thing that is constantly deepening, sometimes faltering, but always capable of being reinforced.

Even when trust is violated, or misunderstandings occur, these are not dead ends. Instead, they can act as a junction. When approached with honesty, empathy, and a genuine willingness to mend, these situations can potentially deepen individuals' trust.

Communication is essential when discussing trust. The lifelines that nourish trust are open channels characterized by transparency and empathy. Trust must be a two-way street, with both parties actively participating in its growth and maintenance.

THE POWER OF PRESENCE

Being present extends beyond physical proximity. It's an emotional and mental immersion into the moment that communicates to the other person that they are truly seen and valued. This level of involvement is essential for establishing deep emotional connections and ensuring that individuals feel not only heard but truly understood.

Genuine presence is a gift in a world full of distractions. It's an assertion that, in that moment, nothing else matters more than the person you're conversing with. This unwavering focus not only promotes comprehension but also communicates respect and validation.

However, being present is not a passive act. Tuning in, discerning underlying emotions, picking up on nonverbal cues, and understanding unsaid words are all required. This level of involvement enables people to face challenges together and find joy in mutual celebrations.

The beauty of presence is that it is not only outwardly focused. People can also be present with themselves, contemplating their feelings and desires. Such introspective moments promote clarity in personal desires and needs, resulting in more genuine interactions with others.

The path to cultivating presence is an ongoing one. It is based on mindfulness and requires people to constantly tune in, recalibrate, and ensure they are truly present, both for themselves and for others.

ACTIVE LISTENING AND VALIDATION

Active listening is more than just hearing. It's a whole-hearted engagement in which one processes not only the spoken word but also the emotions, sentiments, and subtle nuances that accompany it. This kind of nonjudgmental listening is essential for fostering secure attachments because it leads to deep understanding and validation.

While it may appear simple, active listening necessitates a conscious effort. It requires putting personal biases aside, resisting the urge to frame a response while the other person speaks, and truly immersing oneself in the speaker's world. The rewards, on the other hand, are profound, resulting in bonds founded on mutual respect and understanding.

Validation, a subset of active listening, does not imply agreement. Instead, it is about validating another person's feelings and experiences. Such acknowledgment can be extremely empowering, giving people a safe space to express themselves while knowing they will be seen and accepted.

Active listening serves several functions in the web of relationships. It aids in conflict resolution by allowing individuals to understand underlying concerns, as well as strengthening day-to-day interactions by instilling empathy and depth.

Active listening, like most relationship-building practices, is not a one-time event. It is a continuous commitment to see and understand others, requiring both mindfulness and an unwavering desire to connect.

SETTING AND RESPECTING BOUNDARIES

Boundaries are frequently misinterpreted as barriers or walls. They are, however, the guidelines that preserve individuality while fostering mutual respect in the realm of secure attachments. Boundaries communicate one's needs and limits, ensuring that relationships are founded on understanding rather than assumptions.

Setting boundaries is not an act of exclusion, but rather an act of self-respect. Individuals can navigate relationships with clarity and respect if they clearly define what makes them comfortable or uncomfortable. As a result, both parties understand the playing field and can cultivate a bond free of unreasonable expectations.

Setting boundaries, however, is only one side of the coin. Respecting the boundaries set by others is also essential. This adherence respects the autonomy of the other and builds trust, fostering an environment of mutual care and consideration.

It is not always easy to navigate boundaries. Pushback, misunderstandings, or genuine ignorance may occur. When approached with empathy and open communication, these moments provide an opportunity to deepen the relationship by aligning perspectives and expectations.

A boundary-respecting relationship is analogous to two

trees growing side by side. Their roots intertwine, providing mutual support, but they also give each other room to grow, reach out, and thrive on their own.

EMOTIONAL AVAILABILITY AND VULNERABILITY

The willingness to share and engage with one's own and others' emotional experiences is referred to as emotional availability. It is the willingness to be moved, affected, and changed by these interactions. The first step toward emotional availability frequently necessitates an inward journey to understand and accept our emotions without judgment.

In a world that frequently rewards stoicism, vulnerability is brave. It's an invitation to show someone your true self, complete with hopes, fears, and dreams. Vulnerability is a two-pronged act that involves baring one's soul while also being open to another's innermost revelations.

The delicate dance between emotional availability and vulnerability. Both necessitate but also strengthen trust. It's a strange paradox that revealing one's perceived weaknesses can actually be a source of strength in a relationship.

Patience is an important aspect of this dance. Not everyone is prepared to be vulnerable. Recognizing this misalignment without judgment and making room for gradual emotional intimacy opens the door to genuine connection.

Secure attachment thrives in an environment of emotional openness and vulnerability. When people are open, receptive, and genuinely engaged in their relationships, they weave a tapestry of mutual understanding, empathy, and deep connection.

NAVIGATING CONFLICTS CONSTRUCTIVELY

Every relationship, no matter how harmonious, will have disagreements. What distinguishes a securely attached relationship from others is not the absence of conflict but how it is handled. Secure attachment serves as a foundation, ensuring that the underlying bond remains unbroken even when disagreements arise.

Respect is the foundation of constructive conflict resolution. It starts with understanding that disagreements are about mutual understanding and growth, not about winning or losing. Conflicts are transformed from destructive storms into opportunities for deeper connection when viewed through this lens.

Active listening, as previously discussed, is critical in conflict resolution. Furthermore, it is critical to express oneself using "I" statements, which communicate feelings without assigning blame. For example, instead of saying, "You always..." say, "I felt hurt when..."

Knowing when to pause is also an important part of conflict resolution. When emotions aren't as high, taking a step back, reflecting, and re-engaging can provide clarity, leading to more fruitful discussions.

Secure attachment does not guarantee a life free of conflicts. Instead, it provides the tools and the foundation for constructively navigating them, ensuring the relationship grows stronger and more resilient with each challenge.

THE ROLE OF INTIMACY

Intimacy, frequently equated with physical closeness, encompasses a much broader spectrum. Intimacy is fundamentally about deeply knowing and being known. It is the convergence of emotional, intellectual, and physical closeness that serves as the foundation of securely attached relationships.

Individuals can share their deepest thoughts, fears, and dreams through emotional intimacy, which is based on trust, vulnerability, and open communication. This sharing and the resulting understanding demonstrates the bond's strength, in which individuals can be their authentic selves without fear of judgment.

Intellectual intimacy, while less discussed, is just as important. It is the exchange of ideas, dreams, and aspirations. Such interactions stimulate the mind, fostering respect and admiration while also adding depth to the relationship.

Physical intimacy, outside of romantic relationships, is also important. The comfort of a hug, the warmth of a handhold, or the solace of a shoulder all communicate care, comfort, and closeness in a language beyond words.

The dynamic nature of intimacy is its beauty. It grows, deepens, and sometimes needs to be rekindled. Recognizing and nurturing each aspect of the relationship ensures that it remains vibrant, connected, and deeply rooted in mutual understanding and care.

THE IMPORTANCE OF AUTONOMY

While secure attachment values closeness and connection, it also values autonomy. Each participant's uniqueness is recognized and celebrated in a securely attached relationship. It recognizes that in order for a bond to truly flourish, each individual must have the freedom to grow, explore, and be their true self.

Autonomy is not isolation; rather, it is the freedom to pursue one's passions, interests, and dreams while knowing that a supportive partner is cheering from the sidelines. This balance of togetherness and individuality keeps the relationship alive, vibrant, and mutually empowering.

Additionally, autonomy promotes resilience. Individuals who are given the freedom to face challenges, make decisions, and navigate life's ups and downs on their own terms develop a repertoire of experiences and skills that they then bring back to the relationship, enriching it.

A secure attachment understands the interplay of autonomy and connection. It recognizes that, while shared experiences weave the tapestry of the relationship, individual threads – unique experiences, aspirations, and dreams – add color, depth, and strength to it.

Autonomy development necessitates trust, open communication, and mutual respect. It acknowledges that a relationship comprises two distinct individuals and that their individual growth is just as important as their collective journey.

PARENTING WITH
DISORGANIZED ATTACHMENT

RECOGNIZING YOUR TRIGGERS

*P*arenting is a multifaceted journey that combines love, care, and direction. Each stage of this journey presents its own set of challenges, especially for those who have a history of disorganized attachment.

Triggers, which are emotional reactions based on past traumas or experiences, frequently add another layer of complication. These triggers can elicit strong emotions that appear out of proportion to the current situation.

A child's tantrum or rejection, for example, may elicit intense feelings of abandonment or fear in a parent with disorganized attachment. Such reactions can be perplexing unless the underlying triggers are understood.

Understanding one's triggers necessitates a journey into one's emotional past. It involves revisiting past traumas, identifying patterns, and identifying emotional responses that may be out of sync with the current situation.

This introspection frequently reveals the profound impact of past experiences on current reactions. It's an enlightening process that sheds light on seemingly irrational feelings or behaviors.

Recognizing these triggers is a difficult journey. It necessitates a great deal of introspection and self-awareness. Some people find that professional help is extremely beneficial, as therapists or counselors provide the tools and perspectives required to unearth and address these deeply embedded emotional responses.

The ultimate goal of researching triggers is not to eliminate them. Given the depth of some traumas, complete elimination may be unrealistic. Instead, the goal is to become more self-aware, to anticipate potential emotional pitfalls, and to develop effective coping strategies.

This method allows parents to respond to situations with greater clarity and purpose, reducing the possibility of disproportionate reactions.

Understanding one's triggers is an important step toward becoming a more responsive and empathetic parent in the grand scheme of things. When we can navigate our emotional landscape with awareness, we pave the way for more positive interactions with our children, creating a nurturing environment where they can thrive.

BUILDING A SECURE BASE FOR YOUR CHILD

The essence of secure attachment is the creation of an environment that a child perceives as safe and dependable. It is a setting in which a child is consistently valued, understood, and supported.

This type of foundation is critical to their emotional and psychological well-being. This secure foundation is the source of a child's trust in their caregiver, their belief that they can rely on them for love and support.

A secure foundation is built on consistency. It's not just about being physically present, but also about being emotionally available. When a child knows they can count on their caregiver to be there for them in both happy and sad times, it fosters a profound sense of security.

Building consistency may be difficult for parents who have experienced disorganized attachment in their own childhood, but it is all the more important. It gives them the opportunity to provide their child with the stability they may have lacked.

In establishing a secure foundation, open communication complements consistency. It entails actively listening to a child's worries, fears, and hopes.

It entails creating an environment in which they feel comfortable sharing their feelings and opinions, and in which they believe their feelings and opinions are valued. Children learn in this environment that their voice matters and that they are an important part of the family dynamic.

However, creating this safe environment benefits both the child and the parent. It is a journey of healing and breaking cycles for those who have disorganized attachment. It is about recognizing patterns in one's past and consciously choosing a different path.

It is an act of resilience to ensure that their child receives the consistent love and support that they may have desired.

When we consider the significance of a secure foundation,

its impact on a child's overall development becomes clear. It is more than just a safe place; it is the foundation upon which a child builds their worldview, trust in others, and sense of self-worth. Caregivers can lay the groundwork for their child's healthy emotional growth by emphasizing consistent, empathetic parenting.

EMOTIONAL REGULATION FOR PARENTS

Emotional regulation is critical to effective parenting. It is the ability to understand, manage, and express one's emotions appropriately, resulting in interactions marked by stability, understanding, and mutual respect.

A well-regulated emotional response not only prevents misunderstandings but also serves as a model for the child's healthy emotional expression.

Maintaining consistent emotional regulation can be especially difficult for parents who have a history of disorganized attachment. Their past traumas or fears may have an undue influence on their reactions, resulting in emotional responses that appear out of proportion to the situation at hand. Recognizing and addressing these patterns is the first step.

It is about recognizing that one's emotional landscape is intricately linked to past experiences and finding effective ways to navigate it.

Several strategies can be used to cultivate emotional regulation. For example, introspection and mindfulness practices can clarify emotional triggers and responses.

For some, therapeutic intervention becomes invaluable, providing tools and insights that allow them to better manage their emotions. The emphasis is on understanding emotions and expressing them in healthy, constructive ways rather than suppressing them.

Modeling emotional regulation for children is an important aspect of emotional regulation. Children learn by watching their caregivers navigate their emotions with grace and understanding.

They pick up on the nuances of emotional intelligence, recognizing the significance of understanding and expressing their emotions appropriately.

Emotional regulation is more than just managing one's emotions; it's a path to more empathetic and understanding parenting. It is about developing deeper bonds based on mutual respect and understanding.

When parents can effectively regulate their emotions, they create an environment where they and their children can thrive, fostering genuine connections and mutual growth.

ATTACHMENT-INFORMED PARENTING APPROACHES

Attachment theory, a cornerstone in understanding interpersonal relationships, offers invaluable parenting insights. It delves into the complexities of how people form relationships with their caregivers and how these bonds influence future relationships.

An attachment-informed approach to parenting entails using the theory's insights to guide one's parenting strategies, ensuring that they meet the child's attachment needs.

This approach is especially important for people who have a history of disorganized attachment. It serves as a road map, assisting them in understanding their attachment style and its implications.

With this clarity, they can tailor their parenting strategies to foster a secure and understanding environment. It is about acknowledging past wounds and making conscious efforts to heal them through current parenting practices.

Attachment-informed parenting is distinguished by consistency, open communication, and emotional availability. These principles ensure that a child has a trusting relationship with their caregiver and that they can rely on them for support, understanding, and love. It is about providing a setting in which a child feels seen, heard, and valued.

Furthermore, the attachment-informed approach focuses on developing strong bonds. It is about understanding the emotional undercurrents, recognizing unspoken feelings, and proactively addressing them.

When a child knows that their caregiver understands them, even if their words are inadequate, it strengthens their sense of belonging and trust.

Finally, an attachment-informed parenting approach provides a comprehensive blueprint. It gives caregivers the tools and insights they need to parent with empathy and responsiveness.

It is a policy that ensures children grow up in a nurturing environment that prioritizes their emotional well-being, promoting healthy emotional growth and strong interpersonal bonds.

DEALING WITH AMBIVALENCE IN PARENTING

Parenting, with all of its joys and challenges, can elicit feelings of ambivalence at times. This mix of conflicting emotions can be especially pronounced in people with disorganized attachment, where past traumas, fears, or uncertainties may be present.

For example, a child's accomplishment may be tinged with feelings of inadequacy or fear. It's a complicated emotional landscape that necessitates understanding and navigation.

It is critical to understand the origins of ambivalence. It is frequently linked to past experiences or traumas. Individuals with disorganized attachment may experience these mixed emotions as a result of their attachment style, reflecting their own experiences with inconsistent or unpredictable caregiving. Recognizing and addressing these patterns is the first step.

Openly discussing feelings of ambivalence can be therapeutic. Many people find that expressing their feelings, whether to a trusted confidant or a professional, provides clarity.

It's a way to work through these feelings, understand their origins, and find ways to manage them. This communication leads to a deeper understanding and more consistent emotional responses.

Furthermore, self-compassion is essential in dealing with ambivalence. It is critical to recognize that parenting is a complex journey filled with highs and lows.

Ambivalence is natural and does not diminish one's ability as a parent. Instead, they reflect the emotional complexities of parenting, particularly for those with complex attachment histories.

In a broader sense, dealing with ambivalence in parenting entails accepting the full range of emotions that come with the job. It is about comprehending, managing, and expressing these feelings in ways that promote growth, understanding, and connection.

Recognizing and addressing ambivalence allows parents to

pave the way for more consistent, empathetic, and understanding interactions, which benefits both them and their children.

PARENTAL STORIES: TRIUMPHS AND TRIALS

Every parent's journey is a tapestry of joy, challenges, memories, and life lessons. These stories carry the weight of their past but also shine with the hope of what the future can hold, especially for those with disorganized attachment. Let us delve deeper into the stories of Ariana and Max, two such people who navigated their complex emotions and created their own parenting narratives.

Ariana's Odyssey: From Shadows to Sunshine

Ariana grew up in a tumultuous home. Her childhood was marred by memories of neglect and inconsistent love. When she found out she was pregnant, her joy was overshadowed by fear. Will she inadvertently pass on her scars to her child? Ariana turned to therapeutic parenting because she was determined not to let her past define her future.

With each session, she began to unlearn her childhood's negative patterns, replacing them with techniques based on empathy and understanding. Ariana was patient when her child threw tantrums or expressed frustration. In stark contrast to her own childhood, she created an environment in which her child always felt safe expressing emotions. Ariana not only healed her child's potential wounds, but she also began to mend her own. Their bond grew stronger as time passed, based on mutual trust and respect.

Max's Expedition: Confronting the Inner Storm

Max was always the life of the party, charismatic, funny, and seemingly self-assured. But beneath the surface were insecurities caused by an unpredictable childhood filled with mixed signals from caregivers. Those old fears resurfaced when his daughter was born. Will he be able to provide the stability he has lacked? He was determined, but he was ill-prepared.

Max sought therapy after realizing he needed guidance. There, he confronted his childhood traumas, piece by piece. He joined parenting support groups, where he found solace in shared experiences and collective wisdom. Each story, each shared strategy, gave Max the tools he so desperately needed. Max's parenting style evolved over time as he gained knowledge and a support network. He started by creating a home that was predictable, open, and full of unconditional love. Growing up with a solid foundation, his daughter became a testament to the power of self-awareness and growth.

BOTH ARIANA and Max's journeys demonstrate the difficulties that result from disorganized attachment, but they also demonstrate the immense power of resilience, support, and personal growth. While their paths were not without obstacles, their unwavering commitment to providing a better life for their children, supported by professional guidance, reshaped their stories. Their stories inspire, reminding every parent that transformation is always possible with understanding and effort.

SEEKING PROFESSIONAL HELP

WHEN TO SEEK THERAPY

 $\mathcal{M}$ any cultures hold that therapy is a last resort, reserved only for the direst circumstances. This is a dangerous misconception. The truth is that therapy is similar to any other preventive health measure. It is not necessary to wait until a cavity becomes unbearable before visiting a dentist; similarly, emotional and mental discomforts do not need to reach critical levels before seeking help. The indications to see a therapist range from persistently low moods to increased anxiety or consistent patterns of unhelpful behavior.

Individuals may consider therapy for a variety of reasons. Some are triggered by traumatic events, such as unexpected loss or change. Others may be dealing with the complications of chronic mental health conditions. Then there are those who are just looking for clarity, direction, or personal growth. The thresholds vary, but the underlying principle remains: if something feels off, it deserves to be addressed.

Interpersonal relationships can reflect our internal state. Recurring patterns of conflicts, misunderstandings, or emotional disconnect with loved ones or colleagues may indicate underlying issues. It's important to note that even a sense of stagnation in personal growth can be a valid reason to seek therapeutic intervention.

The realization that one requires assistance is not a sign of weakness. It demonstrates self-awareness and strength. Recognizing when one's coping mechanisms have failed or when emotional burdens have become too much to bear is the first step toward recovery.

FINDING THE RIGHT THERAPIST

There are numerous approaches, methodologies, and practitioners in the therapeutic realm. Navigating this landscape can be difficult, but with the right tools and perspective, you can find a therapist who is a good fit for you. Begin by determining what you hope to gain from therapy. Do you want to learn how to deal with anxiety? Insights into behavioral patterns? Or simply a safe haven for expression and exploration?

After you've defined your objectives, start looking for therapists who specialize in these areas. There are now numerous online platforms dedicated to matching people with suitable therapists, complete with reviews and testimonials. While such platforms are a good place to start, don't underestimate the value of personal recommendations. Friends, family, and even primary care providers can be invaluable sources of referrals.

Your first sessions with a therapist are critical. They give you a sense of their approach and whether their demeanor matches yours. It's critical to assess your level of comfort. Vulnerability is required for therapy, and you should be with someone who encourages that openness.

Finances are a factor to consider. Many therapists offer a sliding scale based on income or a set number of sessions at a discounted rate. Some forms of therapy may also be covered by insurance, so it's worth looking into what's available to you.

ATTACHMENT-FOCUSED THERAPY

Attachment-focused therapy is based on the understanding that early relationships, particularly those with primary caregivers, shape our adult behaviors, relationships, and even our sense of self. This approach, based on attachment theory, delves into the bonds formed during infancy and childhood, examining their consequences into adulthood.

Attachment theory's founder, John Bowlby, emphasized the evolutionary nature of attachment behaviors, claiming that children are biologically predisposed to form attachments with caregivers as a means of survival. When these caregivers are consistently available and responsive, children develop a secure attachment style, confident in their attachment figures' availability and support.

Children can develop various insecure attachment styles when caregivers are inconsistent, unavailable, or even harmful. As a result, attachment-focused therapy seeks to investigate and address the consequences of these early attachment experiences. This type of therapy focuses on unraveling, understanding, and, if necessary, reshaping the attachment narratives that people carry with them.

Therapists who use this modality employ a variety of techniques, ranging from traditional talk therapy to more experiential methods. The ultimate goal is to cultivate a secure internal foundation from which individuals can navigate their relationships and the larger world.

GROUP THERAPY AND ITS BENEFITS

Humans are social creatures by nature. We thrive in groups and find solace in shared experiences. Group therapy capitalizes on this inherent human trait by fostering a therapeutic community in which individuals come together to address common challenges or achieve common goals. Group therapy, as opposed to one-on-one therapy, provides a rich tapestry of interactions, insights, and shared healing.

One of the most important advantages of group therapy is the realization of universality. Discovering that one's difficulties, fears, or experiences are not unique can be extremely therapeutic. This shared sense of struggle fosters a strong sense of belonging, which helps to alleviate feelings of alienation or loneliness.

Group therapy, in addition to providing support, holds an individual accountable. Attending sessions on a regular basis and witnessing the progress or struggles of others can be motivating. It is a gentle reminder of one's dedication to healing and growth.

Real-time feedback is also possible due to the group dynamic. It's a place where people can try out new behaviors, communication styles, or coping strategies while learning from the therapist and other group members.

MEDICATION: WHAT TO CONSIDER

While therapy provides a safe space to explore, understand, and address emotional and psychological issues, there are times when medication can be a helpful supplement. Individuals with certain mental health conditions may benefit from psychiatric medications, just as diabetics may require insulin. However, it is critical to approach this path with caution, understanding, and a well-informed viewpoint.

First, it is critical to understand that medication is not a panacea. It frequently works best when combined with therapy. Medication can help to stabilize moods or alleviate certain symptoms, making the environment more conducive to therapeutic work.

It is critical to consult a psychiatrist or primary care provider when considering medication to ensure a thorough evaluation. This includes knowing potential side effects, interactions with other medications, and treatment duration.

Psychiatric medications carry a stigma that stems from misconceptions or generalized views. However, for many, these medications provide a semblance of normalcy, allowing them to function daily. If you go this route, make sure to visit your doctor regularly to monitor any changes or potential side effects.

ALTERNATIVE AND COMPLEMENTARY THERAPIES

In our pursuit of mental and emotional well-being, there is a growing acceptance of therapies that are not traditional therapeutic. Acupuncture and herbal treatments are examples of alternative and complementary therapies.

Also, therapies such as Reiki, a type of energy healing, have gained popularity among those seeking a state of mind-body balance. Then there's aromatherapy, which employs essential oils to elicit specific moods or relieve specific symptoms. Art and music therapies provide outlets for creative expression, exploration, and understanding.

The caveat here is that these therapies should be viewed as complementary. They can be used in conjunction with traditional therapeutic modalities to maximize the benefits. However, before embarking on any alternative treatment path, it is important to consult with a primary care provider to ensure it aligns with your specific needs and does not conflict with any ongoing treatments.

SETTING GOALS FOR THERAPY

Entering therapy without clear goals is akin to setting out on a journey with no destination in mind. Setting goals provides direction and a roadmap for tracking progress. Begin with broad goals. Perhaps you want less anxiety, better relationships, or clarity on your life's purpose.

Working with your therapist, break down these overarching goals into smaller, more tangible objectives. These mini-goals serve as milestones, providing a sense of accomplishment as you progress through therapy.

Furthermore, having clear goals allows for open communication with your therapist. It brings you both together, ensuring that the therapeutic interventions are aimed at your desired outcomes. Revisit and adjust these goals on a regular basis to ensure they remain relevant and reflective of your changing needs.

NAVIGATING CHALLENGES IN THERAPY

Therapy is not a straight line. It's full of ups and downs, revelations and challenges. While breakthrough moments provide profound insights and a sense of accomplishment, the challenges can be discouraging. Perhaps certain sessions leave you feeling more depressed than when you started, or you feel like you've reached an impasse, making no discernible progress.

It's critical to remember the cyclical nature of the therapeutic process at this point. It can be unsettling to delve into deep-seated traumas, unearth repressed emotions, or challenge ingrained beliefs. However, these are frequently necessary phases that pave the way for growth and understanding.

Communication is critical when confronted with such challenges. Discuss your feelings, concerns, or fears with your therapist. They can provide perspective, modify their approaches, or even offer coping strategies. The therapeutic journey, with its ups and downs, exemplifies human resilience, adaptability, and the never-ending quest for healing.

THE HEALING POWER OF THE THERAPEUTIC RELATIONSHIP

A universal truth exists among the various therapeutic modalities, techniques, and approaches: the therapeutic relationship's healing power. This bond, developed over time, serves as the foundation for transformative change.

The therapeutic space's safety, which is free of judgment and full of understanding, allows for vulnerability. And it is precisely from this vulnerability that profound insights emerge. The therapist-client relationship is more than just a business transaction. It's a dynamic dance of mutual respect, trust, and cooperation.

The nuances of this relationship can serve as a microcosm for other relationships, providing insights, highlighting patterns, and acting as a testing ground for new behaviors or communication styles. It's a place that reflects, challenges, and ultimately supports the client's quest for happiness.

BUILDING RESILIENCE

THE NATURE OF RESILIENCE

*A*t its core, resilience refers to an individual's ability to weather life's storms, recover from adversity, and grow stronger as a result of the experience. It's not an innate trait that some people have and others don't; rather, it's a dynamic mix of behaviors, thoughts, and actions that can be nurtured and developed. Consider a bamboo tree swaying in the wind; it bends but does not break, and when the wind dies down, it returns to its upright position, rooted yet flexible.

This metaphor explains the essence of resilience. Just as bamboo does not resist the wind but rather moves with it, resilient people do not deny or avoid adversity but instead face it head-on, drawing on a wellspring of inner strength. But where does this power come from? It is a synthesis of past experiences, current coping mechanisms, and forward-thinking optimism.

Many people mistakenly believe that resilience is about passively enduring, soldiering on without complaint. In reality, emotional agility refers to the ability to navigate one's feelings, seek help when needed, and express oneself authentically. It's about realizing that setbacks are a normal part of life, not an anomaly.

Cultivating resilience is a proactive journey rather than a reactive one. It's similar to building a muscle in that it takes consistent effort, training, and, at times, pushing oneself past perceived limits. Over time, this resilience muscle memory can turn challenges into stepping stones, paving the way for growth.

REFRAMING CHALLENGES

Our perceptions influence our reality. How we interpret events, particularly adversities, can either strengthen or erode our resilience. Reframing is a powerful cognitive tool that involves changing these interpretations and viewing problems through a different, more constructive, and empowering lens.

Consider the concept of failure. The traditional failure narrative is one of defeat, inadequacy, and an endpoint. This narrative could be reframed by viewing failure as feedback, a learning opportunity, and a precursor to eventual success. This shift in perspective does not diminish the disappointment or pain of the setback, but it does change its impact, transforming it from a roadblock to a detour.

Reframing is not about being overly optimistic or denying reality. It is about selecting a viewpoint that promotes one's growth and well-being. It's the difference between wondering, "Why is this happening to me?" and wondering, "What can I learn from this?"

BUILDING A SUPPORT SYSTEM

The poet John Donne correctly wrote that "No man is an island." A strong support system can make all the difference as we navigate the many challenges that life throws at us. This network, which includes family, friends, mentors, and support groups, acts as a safety net, providing emotional support, practical advice, or simply a listening ear.

Developing such a system begins with cultivating relationships, with quality being prioritized over quantity. It's not about having a large social circle but about cultivating deep, meaningful connections with people who share your values and provide mutual support.

Face-to-face interactions have enormous value in an age dominated by digital interactions. Shared experiences, whether they are celebratory or mundane, help to strengthen bonds. They build a reservoir of shared memories that can be drawn on during difficult times.

It's also important to actively participate in this support network, offering help, insights, or empathy when others need it. This type of reciprocity not only strengthens bonds but also reinforces a person's sense of purpose and belonging.

MINDSET SHIFTS FOR GROWTH

A growth mindset, coined by psychologist Carol Dweck, is at the heart of resilience. A growth mindset, as opposed to a fixed mindset, believes that abilities and talents are innate and unchangeable and can be developed through dedication and hard work. This mindset thrives on challenges, viewing them as opportunities for growth rather than impassable barriers.

Recognizing and challenging self-limiting beliefs is part of adopting a growth mindset. These are frequently deep-seated, resulting from previous experiences or societal conditioning. By actively seeking feedback, embracing lifelong learning, and celebrating the journey as much as the outcome, one can cultivate a resilient mindset.

It's also about developing patience and understanding that growth isn't always linear. There will be periods of rapid progress and periods of apparent stagnation. With a growth mindset, however, even plateaus provide insights, shaping one's resilience and determination.

CELEBRATING SMALL WINS

In our goal-oriented culture, it's easy to become fixated on the destination, ignoring the journey's numerous milestones. Celebrating small victories is a deliberate practice that recognizes and revels in incremental progress toward larger goals. This isn't just about boosting morale; it's also an important part of developing resilience.

Every acknowledgment, whether it's completing a task or simply recognizing an internal shift, strengthens one's belief in one's own abilities. It serves as a reminder of progress, particularly during difficult periods when the end goal appears distant or elusive.

These celebrations also create a positive feedback loop. Recognizing a win, no matter how minor, releases dopamine, a neurotransmitter linked to pleasure and motivation. This trains the brain to seek out such victories over time, fostering a proactive and resilient approach to challenges.

EMBRACING VULNERABILITY

Contrary to popular belief, resilience does not imply stoicism or an unwavering display of strength. True resilience includes vulnerability, or the ability to recognize one's own fears, doubts, and uncertainties. Genuine growth occurs as a result of this recognition.

Brené Brown, a well-known researcher and author, refers to vulnerability as the source of innovation, creativity, and change. We foster personal growth and deeper connections with those around us by opening ourselves up, embracing our imperfections, and sharing our authentic experiences.

With its rawness and authenticity, vulnerability challenges societal norms of perpetual positivity and success. It provides a more comprehensive narrative, encompassing the full range of human experiences, both triumphant and challenging. We pave the way for genuine resilience, which is rooted in self-awareness and authenticity, by accepting our vulnerability.

DEVELOPING GRIT AND DETERMINATION

According to psychologist Angela Duckworth, grit is the combination of passion and perseverance toward long-term goals. It is an innate motivation that drives people to persevere in the face of adversity. Grit, like resilience, can be developed and nurtured.

Building grit entails cultivating a strong connection with

one's goals and understanding the underlying 'why' that motivates these ambitions. It is not only about external accomplishments, but also about aligning these accomplishments with personal values and larger life goals.

Furthermore, grit thrives in environments that promote consistency and dedication. It's about showing up every day, regardless of the immediate results. This consistent effort accumulates over time, resulting in significant progress.

SEEKING INSPIRATION: ROLE MODELS AND MENTORS

Throughout history, stories of people who overcame enormous adversity to achieve greatness have inspired countless others. These role models, whether famous or personal acquaintances, provide tangible evidence of resilience and grit in action.

Seeking out such sources of inspiration, whether through biographies, documentaries, or personal interactions, can provide priceless insights. These stories, filled with obstacles, setbacks, and eventual triumphs, serve as road maps, guiding and motivating individuals on their individual journeys.

Mentors are extremely important in this situation. Mentors, as opposed to role models, who may be distant or inaccessible, provide personalized guidance, drawing on their experiences to advise, challenge, and support. A trusting and mutually respectful mentor-mentee relationship can accelerate personal growth by providing clarity and direction.

TOOLS AND TECHNIQUES FOR BUILDING RESILIENCE

Building resilience requires both internal changes and external practices. Journaling, for example, provides a safe space for introspection, allowing individuals to process experiences, identify patterns, and map out growth trajectories.

Mindfulness and meditation practices, which have their roots in ancient traditions, have grown in popularity in recent years. These techniques, which are centered on the present moment, promote emotional agility and provide tools for navigating adversities with calm.

Physical practices, such as regular exercise, yoga, or even simple breathing exercises, can help build resilience. They not only provide physical benefits, but they also promote mental tenacity, discipline, and focus.

THE ROLE OF COMMUNITY AND SOCIETY

SOCIAL INFLUENCES ON ATTACHMENT

*I*t is often said that it takes a village to raise a child, emphasizing the community's collective impact on individual development. Attachment theory, primarily concerned with caregiver-child dynamics, does not work in isolation. It is heavily influenced by the larger societal context. Our societal values, norms, and practices shape how caregivers interact with their children, laying the groundwork for future relational patterns.

Economic factors, for example, can have a significant impact on attachment styles. Poverty-stricken families may struggle to provide consistent care, resulting in insecure attachment patterns in children. Societal events, such as wars or natural disasters, cast a long shadow on individual attachment, frequently introducing trauma into the equation.

However, it is not only about macroeconomic events or socioeconomic contexts. Community beliefs about parenting, discipline, or emotional expression, for example, can subtly guide caregiver behavior. Societies that value stoicism, for example, may discourage emotional expressiveness, potentially influencing attachment dynamics.

Another factor to think about is the impact of community structures and support. Extended families, close-knit communities, or social safety nets can help primary caregivers overcome some of the challenges they face, enriching the attachment environment.

THE ROLE OF EDUCATION AND AWARENESS

Education is a powerful tool for shifting societal paradigms. Raising awareness and providing knowledge about attachment and mental well-being can transform communities from the ground up. Knowledge dispels myths, challenges stereotypes, and equips people to make sound decisions.

Educational initiatives can range from formal school curriculums to community workshops and seminars that incorporate emotional intelligence and mental health. By instilling these topics early on, we can raise a generation that is more aware of their own and others' emotional needs.

Furthermore, educating professionals, such as teachers, healthcare providers, and community leaders, about attachment theory and its implications can have far-reaching consequences. Armed with knowledge and tools, these professionals can then serve as pillars of support, guidance, and change in their communities.

Education is more than just disseminating information; it is also about fostering dialogues. Open discussions, community forums, and support groups can all help to create safe spaces for people to share their experiences, seek guidance, or simply find comfort in collective understanding.

BUILDING SUPPORTIVE COMMUNITIES

At their best, communities serve as safety nets, providing assistance, resources, and a sense of belonging. Supportive communities can make a huge difference in the context of attachment and mental health. Individuals feel seen, heard, and valued in these environments, regardless of their attachment styles or challenges.

Empathy and understanding are essential for building such communities. This could include community-led workshops, peer support groups, or even storytelling sessions where people share their stories. While these stories are unique in their details, they frequently echo universal themes, bridging divides and fostering connections.

Furthermore, tangible resources such as community centers, helplines, and counseling services can provide critical assistance. These resources, especially when easily accessible and affordable, can serve as lifelines for those dealing with attachment or mental health issues.

Collaboration is also important in supportive communities. This could entail bringing together local schools, healthcare providers, businesses, and individuals, pooling resources, and developing holistic support systems. Whether it's mentoring programs, support groups, or well-being-focused community events, collaborative efforts have a greater impact.

POLICY CHANGES AND ADVOCACY

While grassroots movements and individual initiatives are important, systemic change frequently necessitates policy-level interventions. Governments, institutions, and organizations have the ability to effect large-scale changes that affect millions of people. Policy changes can pave the way for a more informed, empathetic, and supportive society when it comes to attachment and mental health.

This could include policies that encourage parental leave, allowing caregivers to bond with their children during the critical first few months. It could also be funding for mental health services, ensuring that those in need have access to high-quality care without incurring exorbitant costs.

Advocacy is critical in this situation. Activists, professionals, and affected individuals can gather to discuss their needs, challenges, and possible solutions. This collective voice, particularly when persistent and well-informed, has the potential to influence policymakers by drawing attention to pressing issues and potential interventions.

However, advocacy is more than just influencing policy. It's also about changing societal perceptions, combating stigma, and cultivating a more welcoming, understanding community ethos. Advocates can drive systemic and grassroots change through campaigns, awareness drives, and educational initiatives.

SOCIAL MEDIA AND ITS INFLUENCE

Social media platforms wield enormous power in the digital age, shaping opinions, perceptions, and behaviors. These platforms provide a double-edged sword in terms of attachment and mental health. On the one hand, they serve as a platform for education, advocacy, and support. On the other hand, they can reinforce myths, amplify insecurities, and even create environments conducive to comparison and judgment.

Several campaigns and movements have used social media to raise awareness about mental health by providing resources, personal stories, and expert insights. With their global reach, these campaigns can potentially normalize mental health conversations, making them part of the mainstream discourse.

However, the curated realities frequently displayed on these platforms can aggravate feelings of inadequacy, isolation, or insecurity. Social media can sometimes amplify attachment issues, particularly those related to self-worth or relational dynamics.

Individuals can, however, harness the positive potential of these platforms by practicing mindful consumption, setting boundaries, and actively seeking supportive online communities. When used with intention and awareness, social media can provide connections, insights, and resources, assisting one's journey toward better attachment and well-being.

DE-STIGMATIZING MENTAL HEALTH

Historically, stigma, misconceptions, and fear have surrounded mental health. Such societal attitudes, while slowly changing, continue to be barriers to seeking help, expressing vulnerabilities, or simply acknowledging one's difficulties. De-stigmatizing mental health is critical for creating a society that genuinely supports attachment well-being.

Open dialogues, both in public and private settings, can chip away at these stigmas over time. Hearing from people who have overcome mental health challenges, understanding their journeys, and recognizing their strengths can help to humanize these experiences and break down stereotypes.

The media, in all of its forms, plays an important role. Media can reshape societal perceptions by showcasing authentic, diverse, and holistic depictions of mental health. This includes highlighting not only challenges, but also recovery, resilience, and the multifaceted nature of the human experience.

Furthermore, as previously mentioned, education remains a cornerstone. We can foster a generation that is more informed, empathetic, and proactive about their mental health by incorporating mental health into mainstream educational curricula.

THE POWER OF COLLECTIVE HEALING

Humans are social beings by nature, drawing strength, comfort, and understanding from communal ties. The process of communities coming together to navigate traumas, challenges, or shared experiences, known as collective healing, amplifies the healing potential inherent in human connections.

Collective endeavors can take many forms. It could be rituals, workshops, support groups, or simply communal gatherings centered on processing, healing, and growth. Individuals can express, connect, and heal in these spaces, which are imbued with empathy, understanding, and collective strength.

Collective healing approaches are especially beneficial for historical or generational traumas that affect entire communities or cultures. These shared experiences, which frequently reverberate across generations, can be processed and healed through collaborative efforts, breaking cycles and fostering resilience.

INITIATIVES MAKING A DIFFERENCE

Across the globe, numerous large and small initiatives are making a real difference in the fields of attachment and mental health. These could be non-profits that provide resources and assistance, community-led movements that raise awareness, or even digital platforms that provide safe spaces for connection and dialogue.

With their on-the-ground insights and community-centered approaches, such initiatives frequently fill gaps left by larger institutional structures. They provide customized solutions that are tailored to the specific needs, challenges, and cultural nuances of their communities.

We not only increase the impact of these initiatives by highlighting and supporting them, but we also draw attention to innovative solutions and models that can inspire and inform other communities. These initiatives, motivated by passion, commitment, and a thorough understanding of community dynamics, demonstrate the power of collective action and the transformative power of community-led change.

THE ROLE OF CULTURE AND TRADITION

Culture and tradition, with their deeply ingrained values, practices, and beliefs, play an important role in shaping attachment dynamics and perceptions of mental health. These cultural differences influence caregiving practices, emotional expression, and even how people seek and receive help.

While cultures often provide a rich tapestry of support, rituals, and community ties, they may also contain beliefs or practices that contradict modern understandings of attachment or mental health. Recognizing these nuances, and utilizing one's strengths while challenging potentially harmful beliefs, is critical for overall well-being.

Cross-cultural attachment studies have highlighted these differences, demonstrating the various ways caregivers around the world interact with their children. While emphasizing universal themes, these insights also highlight the distinct flavors that cultures bring to the attachment tableau.

CHALLENGES ON THE PATH TO HEALING

RECOGNIZING POTENTIAL SETBACKS

*T*he healing journey, while filled with moments of growth and clarity, is not without its challenges. The road to personal betterment and resolution, like any journey, may be littered with potholes and detours. Recognizing potential setbacks not only provides us with the foresight to avoid them, but also softens the blow when they do occur.

Relapse or regression is a common setback. Following a period of progress, old patterns, behaviors, or emotions may resurface. This is a normal part of the healing process and does not negate the progress that has already been made.

Setbacks can also be precipitated by external factors such as environmental stressors or specific events. These triggers may elicit memories of past traumas, complicating our healing and progress.

Expectations, especially rigid or unrealistic ones, can set us up for disappointment. It's critical to understand that healing isn't a straight line. There will be ups and downs, and comparing one's journey to a rigid yardstick can lead to unnecessary heartbreak.

Comparing one's healing path to that of another can lead to feelings of inadequacy or impatience. Every person's journey is distinct, shaped by their experiences, coping mechanisms, and personal timelines.

Finally, physical factors such as health issues or changes in one's environment can have an effect on one's healing process. Recognizing these potential setbacks and incorporating them into one's healing strategy can make the journey easier and less stressful.

THE ROLE OF GRIEF AND LOSS

Grief and loss are natural parts of the human experience, but they can be difficult to overcome on the road to recovery. These emotions can be overwhelming, casting long shadows over our healing journey, whether it's the loss of a loved one, the end of a relationship, or grief stemming from past traumas or missed opportunities.

Grief, in all of its forms, can elicit a wide range of emotions, from rage to sadness, regret to disbelief. Navigating these intense emotions requires patience, understanding, and, in many cases, professional assistance.

Loss can also rekindle feelings of vulnerability, reviving old traumas or insecurities. Such events can be devastating, especially for those already on a healing path.

However, it is critical to recognize that, while grief and loss are undeniably difficult, they also provide opportunities for profound personal growth. They force us to confront our deepest emotions, rethink our priorities, and frequently result in increased empathy and understanding.

It's also worth noting that grief has no set timetable. Some people's feelings may fade with time, while others may experience waves of grief long after the triggering event. It is critical to recognize and respect one's own grieving process.

Community, peer support, and professional therapy can all help you navigate the maze of grief. Sharing one's emotions, seeking solace in shared experiences, or simply having a safe space to express oneself can make all the difference.

DEALING WITH OVERWHELM

On the road to recovery, it is common to feel overwhelmed. This sensation can result from a barrage of emotions, confronting deeply ingrained traumas, or simply the enormity of the healing journey ahead. Dealing with overwhelm, managing it, and preventing it from occurring again becomes critical.

Recognizing the signs of overwhelm is one of the first steps in dealing with it. Anxiety, avoidance behaviors, irritability, or even physical symptoms such as fatigue may result. Being aware of one's own reactions and emotions can provide early warning signs, allowing for timely intervention.

Grounding exercises, such as deep breathing, meditation, or even physical activities, can be extremely effective in dealing with overwhelming feelings. These techniques anchor us, providing a brief respite and clarity in the midst of a storm of emotions.

Setting boundaries with oneself and others can also help to avoid feelings of overwhelm. This could include limiting one's exposure to triggering situations, pacing one's healing journey, or even taking breaks when things become too intense.

Furthermore, breaking down the healing journey into manageable chunks and setting small, attainable goals can make the process appear less intimidating. Celebrating these micro-milestones can provide motivation and a sense of accomplishment.

Friends, family, support groups, and therapists can all be invaluable resources. Sharing one's feelings, seeking advice, or simply having someone to lean on can help relieve the stress of being overwhelmed.

Finally, accepting that feeling overwhelmed is normal and part of the healing process can provide some relief. The journey is about navigating these feelings with grace, patience, and resilience rather than never feeling overwhelmed.

SELF-COMPASSION IN DIFFICULT TIMES

Self-compassion becomes an indispensable ally when navigating the difficult terrains of healing. We are frequently our harshest critics, chastising ourselves for perceived setbacks, comparing our journeys to others, or setting unrealistic expectations. Self-compassion provides a soothing balm in such situations, reminding us of our humanity, worth, and unique journey.

Self-compassion entails treating oneself with the same consideration, understanding, and empathy that one would extend to a close friend. It is accepting that flaws, mistakes, and difficulties are part of the human experience and do not diminish our worth or achievements.

Self-compassion can be practiced simply by reminding oneself of one's strengths, accomplishments, and worth. It's also about recognizing and confronting negative self-talk, those inner critics who exaggerate our flaws and minimize our achievements.

Mindfulness practices such as meditation, journaling, or even deep breathing exercises can help people develop self-compassion. These techniques bring us back to the present moment, allowing us to see our emotions and challenges with detachment and clarity.

The numerous benefits of self-compassion have been consistently highlighted in research, ranging from reduced anxiety and depression to increased resilience and overall well-being. Self-compassion is more than just a feel-good practice; it also has tangible mental and emotional benefits.

Building a self-compassion practice may necessitate outside assistance, especially if one's inner critic is deeply ingrained. Therapists, workshops, and even self-help books can provide insights and tools to help you cultivate this practice.

The understanding that we are all doing our best given our circumstances, experiences, and tools is at the heart of self-compassion. It's a gentle reminder to be kind to oneself, especially during the difficult stages of the healing process.

NAVIGATING RELATIONSHIP CHALLENGES

Healing is, by definition, a deeply personal journey. However, its repercussions frequently extend to our relationships, resulting in challenges, misunderstandings, or even temporary estrangement. Our interactions with others may change as we evolve, heal, and grow, necessitating adaptability, communication, and understanding.

One of the most common issues is a mismatch in healing timelines. While one person may be making rapid progress, their partner or close friend may be on a different path. Impatience, frustration, and even guilt can result from this.

In such cases, open communication becomes critical. Sharing one's emotions, difficulties, and insights can help to bridge understanding gaps, fostering empathy and mutual support. Listening, understanding the other person's journey, and recognizing their unique challenges are also important.

Setting emotional and practical boundaries can also protect relationships during difficult times. This could entail requesting solo healing time, limiting discussions on certain triggering topics, or even requesting joint therapy sessions.

It's also important to invest in joint activities, rituals, or practices that nurture the relationship while providing a break from the intensity of healing. These shared experiences can serve as anchors, reinforcing the bond and providing opportunities for joy and connection.

While relationship challenges can be intimidating, they also provide opportunities for growth. overcoming these obstacles can lead to greater understanding, stronger bonds, and improved communication skills. It is about viewing these challenges as opportunities for growth and deeper connections rather than as insurmountable obstacles.

STAYING MOTIVATED DURING SETBACKS

While setbacks are unavoidable on any journey, they can sap motivation, leading to feelings of despair, frustration, or even a desire to give up. However, staying motivated during these trying times, and rekindling one's passion and drive, is critical for long-term healing and growth.

Remembering the 'why' is one of the most powerful motivators. Reconnecting with the reasons for starting the healing journey, the goals, and the desired outcomes, can provide a renewed sense of purpose. It's about staying focused on the big picture, the long-term goals, even in the face of temporary setbacks.

Setting smaller, more attainable goals can also help to boost motivation. While contributing to the larger journey, these mini-milestones provide moments of accomplishment, celebration, and motivation. They serve as constant reminders of one's progress, potential, and abilities.

Seeking external motivation, whether through inspirational stories, motivational books, workshops, or peer support, can also help to rekindle one's drive. Seeing someone else's journey, challenges, and triumphs can sometimes provide the motivation needed to keep going.

It's also critical to identify and challenge negative self-talk or beliefs that may be undermining motivation. Beliefs such as "I'm not good enough," "I'll never heal," or "It's too difficult" can be self-fulfilling, and challenging them can pave the way for renewed motivation.

Celebrate every progress, no matter how small. Recognizing and rewarding oneself for the strides made, even if they seem minuscule, can offer a motivational boost. It's a reminder that every step, regardless of size, contributes to the larger journey.

Finally, seeking outside assistance, particularly during demotivating periods, can be extremely beneficial. Friends, family, support groups, or therapists can provide perspectives, encouragement, and insights that can propel one forward even in difficult times.

THE ROLE OF PATIENCE AND PERSEVERANCE

On the healing journey, the virtues of patience and perseverance cannot be overstated. Healing is, by definition, a process that can last months, years, or even a lifetime. Navigating this journey necessitates unwavering dedication, deep patience, and the determination to persevere even when the path appears treacherous.

Patience entails acknowledging and respecting one's individual healing timeline. It's realizing that healing isn't a race, and that everyone's path is different, influenced by their experiences, coping mechanisms, and support systems. Patience serves as a gentle reminder that every moment, every challenge, and every emotion is woven into the larger tapestry of healing.

Perseverance, on the other hand, is the driving force, the unwavering spirit that propels one forward even in the face of setbacks, challenges, or doubt. It is steadfast dedication to oneself, one's healing, and one's future.

Patience and perseverance work well together to keep one committed, hopeful, and focused on their healing journey. They serve as anchors, keeping one afloat even in the most violent storms.

Building these virtues may require conscious effort, especially if one's natural tendencies are impatient or easily discouraged. Mindfulness, meditation, and even cognitive behavioral therapy can help to cultivate patience and perseverance.

Individuals who have navigated their healing journeys with patience and perseverance can also provide motivation and insights. Their experiences, trials, and triumphs can serve as beacons, guiding and inspiring others.

Lastly, while patience and perseverance are essential, they do not imply relentlessly pushing oneself or ignoring one's emotions. They emphasize the importance of balancing drive with self-compassion, ambition with self-care, and ensuring a holistic and long-term healing journey.

SEEKING SUPPORT IN DIFFICULT TIMES

Even the most resilient people, those who have an arsenal of coping mechanisms and strategies may require outside assistance during particularly difficult times. Recognizing this need, letting go of inhibitions, and seeking help becomes critical for long-term healing and growth.

Support can take many forms. Friends or family may be those trusted confidantes who offer a listening ear, a shoulder to lean on, or even practical advice for some. Others may find solace, insights, and collective healing in support groups, which bring together people facing similar challenges.

Professional help, such as therapists, counselors, or even coaches, can provide specialized tools, techniques, and perspectives, especially during difficult times. Their knowledge and experience, combined with their objective viewpoint, can pave the way for breakthroughs and renewed clarity.

Seeking help is not a sign of inadequacy or weakness. On

the contrary, it demonstrates a person's dedication to their healing, recognition of the challenges they face, and willingness to use every available resource.

It is also critical to recognize the type of assistance required. While friends and family can provide emotional support, certain issues may necessitate professional intervention. Being aware of one's own needs, emotions, and challenges can help one find the right support system.

Building a diverse support system that provides emotional, practical, and professional assistance can be extremely beneficial. It ensures that the necessary resources are available, regardless of the challenge at hand.

Finally, while seeking assistance, it is also critical to provide it. Being present for others, whether by providing assistance, insights, or simply a listening ear, can be therapeutic, fostering mutual healing and strengthening bonds.

REMEMBERING THE WHY: RECONNECTING WITH PURPOSE

It's easy to lose sight of the 'why,' the initial spark that ignited the healing journey, amidst the challenges, setbacks, and moments of doubt. However, reconnecting with this overarching vision can provide clarity, motivation, and a renewed sense of direction.

Remembering the 'why' entails returning to one's initial goals, aspirations, and desired outcomes. It is about picturing your future self as healed, empowered, and transformed. This visualization can serve as a beacon, guiding you through the difficult terrain of healing.

Journaling can be an extremely useful tool in this endeavor.

Writing down one's emotions, hopes, challenges, and goals can provide clarity and perspective. Rereading these journal entries, especially the early ones, can rekindle one's passion and purpose.

Discussions, whether with close confidantes, support groups, or therapists, can also aid in rediscovering one's purpose. Sharing one's journey, challenges, and goals can provide insights, feedback, and, in many cases, a new perspective.

Many people associate their 'why' with their larger life purpose, their role in the community, or even their spiritual beliefs. Delving into these realms, whether in search of answers or simply reconnecting with these larger themes, can provide profound motivation and clarity.

It's also worth noting that the 'why' may change as one's healing journey progresses. What began as a desire for personal improvement may evolve into a desire to assist others, advocate for a cause, or even share one's story. Being open to this evolution and accepting the shifting contours of one's purpose can lead to a richer and fulfilling healing journey.

OVERCOMING CHALLENGES: PERSONAL TESTIMONIES

Shirley's Story: From Shadows to Light

Shirley was raised in a traumatic environment that left an indelible mark on her psyche. Her father, a stern and unpredictable man, frequently vented his rage on the family. Shirley bore the brunt of his rage, which was sometimes physical but more often emotional and psychological in nature. These harrowing experiences instilled in her feelings of worthlessness and self-doubt. As she grew older, the trauma manifested as anxiety disorders and deep trust issues. Relationships were difficult; Shirley frequently found herself pushing people away, afraid of abandonment or betrayal.

During her college years, she came across a peer support group that changed her life. She met others from similar backgrounds here, and their shared stories gave her a sense of belonging and understanding. Shirley sought therapy with their support. The therapeutic process was difficult, with painful memories and years of suppressed emotions to confront. However, Shirley discovered strength and resilience she had never known she possessed with each session.

Shirley felt compelled to give back after witnessing the transformative power of therapy and peer support firsthand. "Shadows to Light," a support group for survivors of childhood trauma, was founded by her. This initiative aimed to create a safe space for people to share, heal, and support one another. Shirley's transformation from a troubled child to a beacon of hope for many people exemplifies the possibility of healing and the power of channeling one's pain into purpose.

Damon's Odyssey: From Chains to Freedom

Damon's addiction began innocuously enough, with occasional recreational drug use at high school parties. However, as the pressures of life mounted — a difficult college environment, a failed relationship, and the unexpected loss of a close friend — he sought solace in substances. Damon's occasional use turned into dependency, and before he knew it, he was caught up in the vicious cycle of addiction. Multiple stints in rehab provided temporary relief, but relapses were common. His self-esteem was further eroded by society's dismissive gaze and whispers. Shame and guilt became constant companions.

Damon's sister intervened one fateful evening, following a particularly harrowing overdose. She introduced him to a one-of-a-kind rehab facility that took a holistic approach to addiction treatment, addressing not only the physical dependency but also the underlying emotional and psychological triggers. Therapists, counselors, and other addicts in recovery became Damon's new family, guiding, supporting, and holding him accountable.

Damon is now a living testament to the power of holistic healing. He's been sober for five years and has dedicated his time to mentoring people who are struggling with addiction. Damon shares his journey, the pitfalls, the victories, and the lessons learned through workshops, personal counseling, and community outreach. His story serves as a beacon of hope for many, demonstrating that with the right support and unwavering determination, even the most formidable chains can be broken.

Both Shirley and Damon's stories, despite their difficulties, demonstrate the incredible resilience of the human spirit. Their journeys are filled with triumphs, growth, and profound transformation, despite the fact that they are filled with pain. They serve as reminders that, no matter how bleak the situation may appear, with support, determination, and a dash of self-belief, healing is not just a possibility, but a promise waiting to be fulfilled.

THE POWER OF STORYTELLING

THE THERAPEUTIC NATURE OF STORIES

Stories have woven the fabric of our societies, cultures, and individual identities since time immemorial. They transcend geographical boundaries, reverberate through the ages, and strike a deep chord within our psyche. Why is this the case? Stories, at their core, are tools for connecting, empathizing, and sharing human experience.

The therapeutic power of stories stems from their ability to frame our experiences, frame our struggles, and find meaning in the midst of chaos. Hearing or reading a story that mirrors the struggles of someone dealing with attachment issues can be both validating and comforting.

Stories also provide a safe haven. They allow for the distant exploration of emotions, traumas, and experiences, allowing us to process and integrate them without feeling overwhelmed.

This distance can be crucial in healing because confronting trauma directly can be retraumatizing.

In the therapeutic realm, narrative therapy employs the power of storytelling to assist individuals in rewriting their life stories, shifting from a problem-saturated story to one of resilience, growth, and transformation.

Furthermore, stories foster a sense of community. Hearing a story that resonates reduces feelings of isolation. It's a gentle reminder that one's struggles, emotions, or experiences are not unique.

Finally, stories provide hope. Hearing about someone who overcame similar challenges or navigated turbulent emotional terrains and emerged stronger can inspire and guide people on their healing journeys.

SHARING YOUR JOURNEY

Sharing your personal story can be both therapeutic and empowering. It is a process of taking responsibility, recognizing your struggles, celebrating your victories, and learning from your experience.

For many people, the act of sharing begins with acknowledging their own story. This self-awareness can be a transformative step that leads to greater self-awareness and acceptance. Journaling, writing letters to oneself, or even speaking aloud in private can be the first steps in this journey of personal storytelling.

Sharing with close confidantes can be the next step once you're ready. Sharing in a safe and supportive environment can lead to validation, insights, and, in many cases, shared narratives. It also encourages deeper connections because vulnerability often opens the door to more authentic relationships.

Choosing more public platforms, such as support groups, workshops, or even online forums, can help to spread the word about your story. It serves as a mirror for others' struggles, challenges, and victories, promoting collective healing.

Sharing also has a cathartic component. Vocalizing or writing down one's journey can help to release pent-up emotions, clear up confusions, and give one's experiences a tangible structure.

However, sharing necessitates tact and discernment. It is critical to choose supportive, respectful, and empathetic environments and listeners. After all, one's story is a deeply personal testament, complete with vulnerabilities, emotions, and lessons.

LEARNING FROM OTHERS' STORIES

As therapeutic as sharing can be, there's equally profound healing potential in listening to and learning from others' stories. These narratives, whether similar or vastly different from one's own, offer a rich tapestry of emotions, experiences, and insights.

Listening to others fosters empathy. It expands one's horizons, offers diverse perspectives, and nurtures a deeper understanding of the myriad human experiences. It's a reminder of the collective human journey, with its shared emotions, struggles, and triumphs.

Furthermore, others' stories can be invaluable guides, especially for those navigating similar challenges. They offer tangible tools, strategies, and coping mechanisms, tested in the crucible of real-life experiences.

In the context of attachment issues, hearing others articulate their feelings, challenges, or experiences can lead to personal epiphanies. It might offer the vocabulary or clarity one was seeking to define their own emotions or experiences.

Books, documentaries, or podcasts centered around personal narratives can be particularly enlightening. They offer deep dives into individual journeys, complete with the nuances, contexts, and reflections.

Additionally, there's comfort in shared narratives. Knowing that someone else has felt, endured, or triumphed over similar challenges diminishes feelings of isolation and offers hope.

THE ROLE OF ART AND CREATIVITY

Art and creativity, in their various manifestations, provide unique platforms for storytelling. They capture the essence of human experiences through colors, movements, sounds, or words, often articulating emotions that are too profound or complex for mere words.

Art becomes a sanctuary for many people, a place where they can explore, express, and even exorcise their emotions. Painting, music, dance, or any other art form can be therapeutic in and of itself, providing both a distraction and a medium for expression.

Art also transcends linguistic barriers. A piece of music, a painting, or a dance performance can resonate with people from all over the world, echoing shared human emotions and experiences.

Making art in the context of attachment issues can provide

a nonverbal medium for processing and expressing complex emotions. It can serve as a mirror, reflecting one's inner world, and this can lead to insights, realizations, and healing.

Furthermore, art gives one's story a physical form. Making something, whether it's a poem, a song, or a sketch, shapes one's experiences, making them more accessible and less overwhelming.

Finally, as with any other form of storytelling, sharing art fosters connections. It allows viewers or listeners into one's world, resulting in empathy, understanding, and, in many cases, shared narratives.

WRITING AS THERAPY

Writing, as a form of expression, has enormous therapeutic potential. It provides a structured, reflective environment to process emotions, experiences, and thoughts. Writing can be especially enlightening for those dealing with attachment issues, providing clarity, catharsis, and a tangible narrative.

Journaling, for example, is an effective self-reflective tool. It is a conversation with oneself that is free of judgments, expectations, or interruptions. Regular journaling can lead to greater self-awareness, pattern recognition, and personal growth over time.

Furthermore, writing provides a safe distance. Writing down traumatic experiences, overwhelming emotions, or tumultuous thoughts acts as a buffer, allowing one to process them without becoming completely immersed in them.

Structured writing exercises, which are commonly used in therapeutic settings, can also help to guide one's journey.

Prompts, reflections, and guided narratives can provide guidance, resulting in deeper insights and healing.

While memoir writing is more involved, it can be a profound experience. Structuring one's life story, recognizing themes, celebrating victories, and learning from setbacks provides both a broader perspective and a tangible narrative. Whether with close confidantes or a larger audience, sharing one's writings can lead to validation, shared experiences, and a sense of belonging.

PODCASTS, FILMS, AND MEDIA ON ATTACHMENT

Multimedia platforms have emerged as powerful storytelling tools in the digital age. Podcasts, films, documentaries, and other forms of media provide diverse, rich narratives that resonate with a global audience.

Podcasts, with their intimate, conversational format, can have a significant impact. They provide in-depth explorations of personal narratives, expert insights, and structured guidance. Podcasts can provide both information and inspiration to those seeking understanding or coping mechanisms for attachment issues.

Films and documentaries can be deeply moving due to their visual storytelling. They provide a broader context by intertwining personal stories with societal, cultural, or historical backdrops. This holistic viewpoint can be illuminating, providing both a micro and macro view of attachment issues.

Furthermore, online platforms such as YouTube and other streaming services have democratized storytelling. They provide a variety of voices, narratives, and perspectives, allowing information and insights to be shared with a global audience.

However, while these platforms provide rich narratives, caution is required. It is critical to select content that is authentic, informed, and respectful. Misinformation or exaggerated narratives can cause more harm than good, resulting in misconceptions, stigmas, or triggers.

INSPIRING MEMOIRS AND BIOGRAPHIES

Memoirs and biographies provide intimate glimpses into people's lives. These detailed narratives, based on real-life experiences, triumphs, setbacks, and reflections, can be especially motivating for those on the road to recovery.

Reading about someone who has overcome similar challenges can be both validating and guiding for those dealing with attachment issues. These memoirs provide concrete coping mechanisms, strategies, and insights, all of which have been tested in the crucible of real-life experiences.

Moreover, biographies provide a broader perspective. They intertwine personal narratives with societal, historical, or cultural contexts to provide a comprehensive picture of the individual's journey.

The authenticity of these stories is what gives them their power. They are not afraid of flaws, setbacks, or challenges. Instead, they provide a raw, unfiltered perspective that is relatable, moving, and deeply resonant.

Additionally, memoirs and biographies provide hope. They are examples of human resilience, perseverance, and growth, serving as beacons for those navigating the perilous terrains of healing.

THE COLLECTIVE NARRATIVE

Each individual story, with its distinct emotions, experiences, and lessons, adds to the larger collective narrative. This shared narrative, woven from many personal narratives, defines cultures, societies, and epochs.

Understanding this collective narrative provides a more comprehensive perspective. It aids in recognizing patterns, shared experiences, and societal influences, resulting in a more comprehensive view of individual experiences.

Recognizing societal, cultural, or generational patterns in the context of attachment can be illuminating. It clarifies external influences, aids in distinguishing between personal and shared challenges, and fosters a sense of belonging.

Contributing to this collective narrative is also empowering. Every shared story, insight, or experience adds to this collective narrative, promoting collective growth, understanding, and healing.

THE HEALING POTENTIAL OF SHARED EXPERIENCES

Shared experiences, whether happy or sad, have tremendous healing power. They alleviate feelings of isolation, provide validation, and promote connections. These shared narratives can be pillars of strength and sources of guidance in the journey of healing from attachment issues.

Recognizing oneself in another person's story provides clarity and validation. It serves as a tangible reminder that one's emotions, experiences, and challenges are not isolated anomalies, but rather shared human experiences.

Furthermore, shared experiences strengthen bonds. They pave the way for more authentic, deeper relationships founded on empathy, understanding, and shared experiences.

Group therapies frequently use the healing power of shared experiences in therapeutic settings. With their shared emotions, challenges, and insights, these collective narratives promote collective healing, growth, and transformation.

LOOKING AHEAD

RECOGNIZING GROWTH AND PROGRESS

*T*aking time to reflect on how far you've come is essential in any healing journey. Growth, particularly in the realms of mental and emotional well-being, is often gradual and can appear almost imperceptible daily. Looking back, on the other hand, can often reveal significant changes that have occurred over longer time periods.

Our memories, influenced by our current emotions, frequently fail to provide a comprehensive picture of our progress. As a result, keeping journals, checking in on a regular basis, or simply having reflective conversations with close friends or therapists can shed light on the subtle but significant changes we go through.

Even minor achievements must be celebrated. Perhaps you responded differently to a trigger, or perhaps you found strength in a vulnerable moment. Recognizing these moments reinforces positive behavior and helps to solidify the lessons learned.

Also, acknowledging progress encourages further development. It inspires by providing tangible evidence that change is not only possible but is already taking place. This type of positive reinforcement can help one continue their journey with renewed vigor.

However, it is critical to approach this reflection with compassion rather than judgment. Progress is not a straight line, and there may be periods of stagnation or even regression. Recognizing growth also entails understanding that each stage, regardless of its nature, contributes to the overall journey.

Finally, celebrating growth, whether by sharing it with loved ones, treating oneself, or simply pausing to be grateful, anchors it, making it more real and palpable.

SETTING FUTURE GOALS

After a certain amount of time has passed in the healing process, looking ahead and setting future goals becomes the next logical step. Setting future intentions provides direction, purpose, and a renewed sense of motivation.

Setting goals should be approached with caution. These are not rigid success indicators, but rather guiding stars that point the way. Being overly strict may result in unnecessary pressure, potentially impeding the organic nature of personal growth.

Setting broad objectives is also critical. While specific goals such as attending therapy sessions on a regular basis or journaling every day are beneficial, broader goals such as 'being more in tune with my emotions' or 'building stronger connections' provide a broader perspective.

Setting these goals with the help of professionals, mentors, or supportive friends can provide clarity and perspective. External input can sometimes shed light on areas that we might otherwise overlook.

Equally important is the process of revisiting and recalibration of these goals regularly. Our needs and aspirations change as we grow, evolve, and change. Changing our goals to reflect where we are now is both realistic and adaptive.

Setting smaller, more attainable targets alongside longer-term goals can be extremely effective. These serve as immediate motivators and provide frequent examples of achievement, fueling the journey forward.

Remember that the point of setting future goals is to strive for personal growth, understanding, and well-being rather than a specific outcome.

EMBRACING THE JOURNEY, NOT JUST THE DESTINATION

It's easy to become fixated on a distant end goal in the pursuit of healing and growth. True fulfillment and understanding, however, often lie in embracing the journey itself, with all of its ups and downs, rather than just a distant destination.

Every stage of the journey, even the difficult ones, teaches us something. Difficulties teach perseverance, patience, and the art of seeking assistance. Gratefulness, presence, and the beauty of connection are all taught by joyful moments. We can gain wisdom from each moment if we embrace it.

Being present in the journey also fosters a stronger connection with oneself. It promotes self-awareness, reflection, and understanding of one's changing needs, aspirations, and emotions.

A journey-focused mindset also promotes adaptability. We become more open to alternative paths, insights, and learnings when not rigidly attached to a specific outcome. This fluidity frequently leads to richer experiences and deeper growth.

It's also worth noting that destinations frequently change. As we evolve, so do our aspirations and perceptions of what it means to be healed or successful. Embracing the journey allows us to remain fulfilled in the face of shifting goalposts.

We cultivate a sustainable source of motivation by finding joy and value in the journey. Instead of being solely motivated by distant goals, daily experiences, insights, and growth become powerful propellants.

Finally, it is critical to recognize that each person's journey is unique. Comparing one's path to that of another can often cause unnecessary stress. Embracing one's journey means appreciating its individuality, pace, and lessons.

CONTINUING EDUCATION AND AWARENESS

The field of mental and emotional well-being is vast and ever-changing. Continuing education and staying informed about new insights, research, and practices can greatly enhance one's healing journey.

Reading books on a regular basis, attending workshops, or even participating in online forums can provide new perspectives and tools. Different modalities, insights, or practices may resonate with us as we grow, opening up new avenues for exploration.

Furthermore, understanding the larger context, whether it is societal trends, new research, or global movements, can provide a more complete picture of one's personal journey. It aids in distinguishing between personal and externally influenced challenges.

Continuous education also provides the ability to make informed decisions. Knowledge is indeed power, whether it is used to select a new therapeutic method, adjust coping mechanisms, or even understand one's evolving emotional landscape.

In today's digital age, we have access to a wealth of information at our fingertips. While this is extremely valuable, it is also critical to approach this information with caution. Using credible sources and remaining open to professional consultation ensures that the information is a genuine asset.

Sharing this knowledge within one's community can also promote collective growth. It could be reading a book together, starting a discussion, or even forming a small study group. Collective exploration frequently results in deeper insights and shared growth.

Finally, it is critical to approach continuous learning with curiosity and openness, rather than obligation. The goal is to enrich and empower oneself rather than overwhelm oneself.

BUILDING HEALTHY RELATIONSHIPS

Relationships, both with oneself and with others, are critical in the healing process. Building and nurturing healthy relationships can significantly aid personal development by providing support, reflection, and joy.

Understanding and establishing personal boundaries is essential for developing healthy relationships. These emotional and physical boundaries ensure mutual respect, understanding, and care. They also safeguard one's energy, ensuring that interactions and connections are nurturing.

Another pillar is effective communication. The ability to express one's feelings, needs, and concerns openly reduces misunderstandings. It also promotes deeper connections based on genuine understanding and empathy.

It is also necessary to recognize and break patterns. Past experiences, particularly in the realm of attachment, frequently have an impact on current relationships. Being aware of these patterns, understanding their origins, and working consciously to break or modify them can lead to healthier relationships.

Mutual development should also be prioritized. At their best, relationships are partnerships in development. Supporting each other's journeys, learning together, and celebrating mutual milestones can all help to strengthen the bond.

However, it is critical to recognize that not all relationships are beneficial to one's well-being. Letting go of toxic or draining relationships is sometimes necessary for personal well-being. It's a difficult but often necessary step in the journey.

Building healthy relationships requires time and effort. Regular check-ins, shared activities, or even relationship 'audits' regularly can keep the connection alive, genuine, and nurturing.

Finally, recognize that every relationship, with its dynamics, challenges, and joys, teaches us something. Accepting these lessons, even from difficult interactions, can promote personal growth and deeper interpersonal understanding.

INVESTING IN PERSONAL WELL-BEING

While external support, whether from relationships, communities, or professionals, is invaluable, investing in one's own well-being ensures that the healing journey's foundation remains strong.

This investment frequently begins with self-awareness. Checking in with oneself regularly, understanding one's current emotional, physical, and mental states, and recognizing one's needs and aspirations, keeps one aligned and grounded.

Developing and sticking to self-care routines can significantly improve well-being. Meditation, physical activity, journaling, and even periodic digital detoxes are anchors, providing stability and grounding.

Furthermore, as previously discussed, investing in continuous learning and growth is an investment in personal well-being. It ensures one has the tools, knowledge, and insights required for the journey.

Prioritizing mental health is also critical. Regular therapy sessions, mindfulness practices, or even simply maintaining a strong support system can help to keep mental health at the forefront.

Physical health, often inextricably linked to mental well-being, should also be prioritized. Regular physical activity, a healthy diet, and enough rest ensure that the body remains a supportive vessel for the journey.

Financial well-being, while often overlooked, is critical. Financial stress can frequently stifle personal development. Investing in financial education, planning, and well-being can help remove potential impediments to healing.

Finally, this investment must be approached with flexibility and kindness. Needs change, and routines may need to be adjusted, which is perfectly fine. The goal is consistent growth and well-being rather than rigid adherence to predetermined patterns.

BEING AN ADVOCATE FOR OTHERS

After overcoming personal obstacles and embarking on a healing journey, one is frequently uniquely positioned to advocate for others. This advocacy can take many forms, but the essence is to use one's insights, experiences, and learnings to help and uplift others.

As previously discussed in the context of storytelling, sharing one's journey is a powerful form of advocacy. It provides encouragement, insights, and tangible evidence of the transformative power of perseverance and support.

Furthermore, using one's voice to spread awareness, challenge stigmas, and foster understanding, whether through platforms, communities, or even one-on-one interactions, can have a significant impact on the journeys of others.

Another way to advocate is to support initiatives, whether they are community-based support groups, global mental health movements, or local workshops. These initiatives frequently provide the structure, resources, and reach needed to supplement individual efforts.

Mentorship can also be a highly rewarding form of advocacy. Guiding, supporting, and sharing with someone earlier in their journey promotes mutual growth and deep, meaningful connections.

Being an active listener can be the most effective form of advocacy. Offering a nonjudgmental, sympathetic ear can provide enormous relief and support, making a real difference in someone's journey.

However, while advocating for others, it is critical to maintain personal boundaries and prioritize one's own well-being. Advocacy should empower and enrich rather than drain and overwhelm.

Finally, it is critical to understand that every bit counts. The smallest gestures, words, or actions can sometimes have the most profound impact. Advocacy begins with being genuine, empathetic, and supportive.

CELEBRATING THE BEAUTY OF HEALING

The healing journey, with all of its challenges, insights, and transformations, is inherently beautiful. Celebrating the beauty of the journey, both the highs, and lows, makes it more fulfilling and meaningful.

Every challenge overcome, every insight gained, and every milestone attained demonstrates the resilience, adaptability, and strength of the human spirit. Recognizing and celebrating these occasions promotes gratitude and motivation.

Also, celebrating the beauty of healing is about more than just personal achievements. Recognizing and celebrating the accomplishments, insights, and growth of others fosters a sense of community and collective upliftment.

It's also critical to see the beauty in the difficulties. While difficulties are inherently unpleasant, they frequently contain profound lessons, insights, and growth opportunities. Accepting and celebrating these obstacles as necessary parts of the journey promotes a holistic understanding of healing.

Making rituals out of these occasions can help to make them

more tangible and meaningful. It could be a personal ceremony, a shared activity with loved ones, or simply a moment of silence.

Sharing these occasions with loved ones, communities, or even larger audiences increases their impact. It provides motivation, hope, and a sense of shared accomplishment.

Finally, understanding that the journey of healing is an ongoing dance of challenges, growth, understanding, and transformation, and celebrating each step, enriches the journey and increases the value of the destination.

PREPARING FOR FUTURE CHALLENGES

While it is important to celebrate growth and healing, it is also important to recognize that challenges will continue to emerge. Preparing for these future challenges ensures one's resilience, adaptability, and empowerment.

Anticipating potential challenges based on previous experiences, patterns, or current circumstances allows one to better equip oneself. Having tools, support systems, or coping mechanisms in place can significantly reduce the impact of these challenges.

Regular check-ins, whether through personal reflections, discussions with therapists, or even feedback from close friends and family, can provide insights into potential problems. Recognizing early warning signs or triggers ensures that responses are proactive rather than reactive.

It is critical to establish and maintain a strong support system. Knowing that there are people, communities, or professionals to lean on during difficult times provides a safety net that strengthens resilience.

Moreover, as previously discussed, continuous learning and growth prepare one for future challenges. When navigating difficulties, new tools, insights, or practices can be extremely beneficial.

Another important factor is mental and emotional agility. Cultivating a mindset that sees difficulties as opportunities for growth, learning, and understanding can change the nature of these difficulties.

Finally, the foundation is trusting oneself, the journey, and the lessons learned thus far. This trust ensures that no matter what challenges arise, one remains anchored, hopeful, and empowered.

THE ONGOING JOURNEY: EMBRACING THE FUTURE WITH HOPE

Healing, growth, and personal understanding are all ongoing journeys. With hope, optimism, and an open heart, we can ensure this journey remains fulfilling, enriching, and trans-formative.

Recognizing that the future, with all of its unknowns, possibilities, and challenges, is a continuation of the current journey provides continuity and perspective. Today's discoveries, insights, and growth lay the groundwork for tomorrow's adventures.

Staying connected to one's purpose, the 'why' of the journey, provides direction and motivation. While this purpose may evolve, it serves as a guiding light, illuminating the path ahead.

Investing in oneself continues to ensure that one is equipped and energized for the journey ahead, whether through education, self-care, relationships, or personal exploration.

Also, knowing that the future will bring both challenges and joys, and being prepared for both, provides a sense of balance. A holistic, enriching journey is ensured by celebrating the joys, learning from the challenges, and finding meaning in both.

Keeping in touch with supportive communities, whether they are therapy groups, online forums, or personal support systems, provides a sense of belonging, understanding, and shared growth.

Finally, looking forward with hope does not imply blind optimism. It's about believing in oneself, the journey thus far, the support systems in place, and the inherent potential for growth, understanding, and transformation. It's about approaching the unknown with curiosity, openness, and a genuine belief in the journey's beauty.

CONCLUSION

REFLECTIONS ON THE JOURNEY

As we near the end of our attachment journey, it's important to take a moment to reflect on where we've been. It has been a transformative journey of insight and growth, from understanding the complexities of attachment to unraveling the nuances of healing.

Every person's attachment experience is unique, shaped by their personal history, relationships, and environment. Yet there are universal threads of connection, longing, and the innate human desire for understanding and intimacy.

The journey also emphasized the significance of early life experiences. These formative years frequently shape our attachment styles, influencing our interactions, relationships, and even inner dialogues for many years to come.

The journey, however, revealed the incredible power of awareness, healing, and transformation. Realizing that one's past does not have to dictate one's future and that healing and change are possible provides enormous hope.

The journey provided a holistic understanding of attachment, its implications, and the paths to healing through personal stories, research, and shared experiences.

Furthermore, the journey emphasized the value of community, support, and shared understanding. Recognizing that one is not alone, that there are resources, communities, and people who understand, can be extremely reassuring.

Finally, reflecting on this journey serves as a reminder that understanding oneself, one's patterns, needs, and aspirations is a never-ending process. It's a dance of introspection, growth, challenge, and transformation, with each step bringing with it its own set of lessons and insights.

THE UNIVERSALITY OF ATTACHMENT STRUGGLES

Attachment is a common human experience. The innate human longing for connection, understanding, and intimacy is consistent regardless of culture, geography, or background.

While the nuances may differ, the core attachment experiences of joy, pain, longing, and understanding are shared by all humans. This universality provides a sense of shared human experience, breaking down isolation or alienation barriers.

In addition, the difficulties associated with attachment, such as feelings of abandonment, difficulties in forming connections, or a desire for deeper understanding, are shared. Recognizing this common struggle fosters empathy, understanding, and a stronger sense of community.

This universality also emphasizes the significance of understanding attachment. As a fundamental human experience, its ramifications permeate all aspects of life, influencing relationships, self-perception, and even broader societal dynamics.

The universality of attachment struggles provides hope. Recognizing that countless others have faced similar challenges, found paths to healing, and formed deeper bonds provides hope and possibility.

It also instills a sense of accountability. Recognizing the universality of these struggles highlights the importance of creating supportive environments, raising awareness, and establishing communities of understanding and healing.

Finally, accepting this universality is an invitation to compassion, both for oneself and for others. Understanding that everyone struggles with attachment issues in their own way fosters greater empathy, patience, and connection.

THE POWER OF KNOWLEDGE AND INSIGHT

One thing became abundantly clear throughout this investigation: knowledge is transformative. Understanding the complexities of attachment, its implications, and the paths to healing enables people to navigate their difficulties more effectively.

This knowledge, which is based on research, personal experiences, and shared insights, serves as a guidepost. It provides guidance, clarity, and a framework for understanding one's own experiences, feelings, and patterns.

The insights gained from this knowledge promote awareness. Recognizing one's patterns, triggers, and needs enables more conscious, informed choices, which pave the way for healing and growth.

Knowledge also dispels myths, misconceptions, and stigmas. Understanding attachment difficulties as a universal human experience, rather than a personal flaw, can be extremely liberating.

Individuals who are well-informed are better positioned to seek out the appropriate resources, support systems, and interventions. It ensures that the path to healing is founded on knowledge rather than trial and error.

This understanding also improves communication. Being able to more effectively articulate one's experiences, feelings, and needs leads to deeper connections, understanding, and support.

Finally, ongoing exploration and learning in the realm of attachment and beyond ensures that one is equipped, informed, and empowered for the journey ahead.

GRATITUDE FOR GROWTH

As with any transformative journey, cultivating gratitude is essential. Recognizing and being grateful for one's growth, insights, and transformations along the way enriches the journey.

Every obstacle overcome, every insight gained, and every milestone reached on this journey demonstrates the human spirit's resilience and adaptability. Gratitude for these moments promotes positivity, motivation, and a greater appreciation for the journey.

Furthermore, gratitude for support systems, whether therapists, loved ones, communities, or even oneself, emphasizes their significance. It promotes stronger bonds, appreciation, and a genuine sense of belonging.

Gratitude also provides context. Recognizing how far one has come, the challenges overcome, and the growth gained provides a broader perspective of the journey, balancing out temporary setbacks or challenges.

Moreover, gratitude magnifies positive experiences. Celebrating and being genuinely grateful for the joys, connections, and understanding gained increases their impact.

Gratitude also encourages resilience. Recognizing and appreciating past growth and transformations prepares and motivates individuals to face future challenges with optimism and hope.

Finally, cultivating a regular gratitude practice, whether through reflection, journaling, or even shared expressions, ensures that it becomes an integral part of the journey, enriching each step.

ACKNOWLEDGING PERSONAL STRENGTH

While support systems, resources, and communities are invaluable, it is also critical to recognize one's own strength. Recognizing and celebrating one's resilience, adaptability, and perseverance helps to empower the journey.

Every person navigating the complexities of attachment demonstrates tremendous strength. It takes courage and determination to confront past traumas, challenge ingrained patterns, and forge new paths of understanding.

Furthermore, acknowledging one's own strength boosts one's self-esteem and confidence. Recognizing one's resilience and adaptability to navigate challenges, grow, and transform oneself boosts self-belief.

In addition, celebrating personal victories, no matter how minor, emphasizes this strength. Every insight gained, every challenge overcome, and every connection made demonstrates personal strength and determination.

This acknowledgement provides motivation as well. Recognizing one's own strength motivates one to keep exploring, understanding, and growing, even when faced with difficulties.

Furthermore, sharing these acknowledgements with loved ones, therapists, or communities increases their impact. It encourages communal celebration, shared motivation, and deeper connections.

Lastly, embracing personal strength does not diminish the value of support systems. Instead, it enhances them. Recognizing one's own strength while also appreciating the available support and resources ensures a balanced, empowered journey.

EMBRACING THE POTENTIAL OF THE HUMAN SPIRIT

The journey of understanding and healing attachment demonstrates the human spirit's incredible potential. Even in the face of adversity, the capacity for growth, understanding, transformation, and connection is nothing short of remarkable.

Accepting this possibility ensures that the journey is approached with hope, curiosity, and an open heart. Recognizing that everyone has the potential for profound transformation and growth is liberating.

Furthermore, this potential is not fixed. With each challenge, insight, and experience, it evolves, grows, and deepens. Embracing the journey's dynamic nature ensures that it remains vibrant, enriching, and fulfilling.

Recognizing potential in others also fosters deeper connections, empathy, and support. Understanding that each individual, with their own set of challenges and experiences, possesses this incredible potential for growth and connection deepens mutual understanding.

This acknowledgement provides hope as well. Recognizing the human spirit's limitless potential serves as a guiding light of hope, motivation, and possibility, even in difficult times.

Also, cultivating environments that nurture this potential, whether in personal spaces, relationships, or communities, ensures that it is fully realized. Supportive, understanding, and empowering environments enhance the potential of the human spirit, fostering growth, connection, and transformation.

Embracing this potential necessitates ongoing exploration, growth, and understanding. Recognizing the limitless potential of the human spirit ensures that the journey is a continuous dance of insight, transformation, and connection.

THE WIDER IMPLICATIONS OF HEALING ATTACHMENT WOUNDS

The path to understanding and healing attachment is not solely personal. Its ramifications span relationships, communities, and even larger societal dynamics.

Deeper personal connections are fostered by healing attachment wounds. Individuals who have gained understanding and insight can form deeper, more meaningful relationships, enriching their lives and the lives of those around them.

These personal transformations have an impact on communities. Individuals who are supportive and understanding foster similar environments, ensuring that communities are more empathetic, cohesive, and connected.

Additionally, the societal implications are enormous.

Understanding and healing attachment challenges breaks the cycle of trauma, misunderstanding, or disconnect, promoting more harmonious and understanding societies.

These implications also highlight the importance of broader awareness, education, and support. The importance of understanding and healing attachment in society fosters environments, policies, and resources that support this journey.

Moreover, the effects of individual healing are multigenerational. Individuals who successfully navigate their attachment challenges ensure that future generations have understanding, resources, and a foundation of connection and intimacy.

Finally, acknowledging these broader implications calls for collective responsibility. It is critical for collective growth, understanding, and harmony to ensure that societies, communities, and relationships support and nurture the journey of understanding and healing attachment.

A CALL TO ACTION: SUPPORTING OTHERS

While personal exploration and healing are important, so is supporting others on their journeys. Being a source of support, understanding, and resources for others enriches both their and one's own journey.

This assistance can take many forms. It could be as simple as active listening, providing resources, sharing personal insights, or simply being a nonjudgmental, empathetic presence.

Creating environments that foster understanding, support, and connection, whether in personal spaces, relationships, or communities, is critical. Such settings make everyone feel seen, heard, and understood.

Also, advocacy is essential. Promoting the value of understanding and healing attachment, advocating for resources, and breaking down stigmas raises awareness and support.

Being open about one's journey, challenges, and insights can help others. Sharing personal stories fosters connection, understanding, and a sense of common humanity.

Ongoing learning, exploration, and growth ensure that the assistance provided remains relevant, informed, and genuine. Being well-versed in knowledge, resources, and insights ensures that one remains an effective support pillar.

Realize that, helping others is not solely altruistic. It deepens connections, fosters shared growth, and fosters a genuine sense of community and belonging.

FINAL WORDS OF ENCOURAGEMENT AND HOPE

As we wrap up this investigation, it's important to leave with words of encouragement and hope. Remember that the path to understanding and healing attachment is one-of-a-kind, transformative, and deeply personal. It is, however, a shared human experience, full of potential, growth, and profound connections.

Accept the journey with an open heart, insatiable curiosity, and genuine optimism. Recognize and celebrate your progress, insights, and transformations. Remember that every challenge provides an opportunity for growth, that every setback is only temporary, and that every insight enriches the journey.

In addition, rely on support systems, whether they are therapists, loved ones, communities, or even personal resources. They enrich the journey by providing understanding, insights, and shared experiences.

Finally, never forget the incredible power of the human

spirit. Even in the face of adversity, the capacity for growth, transformation, connection, and profound understanding is limitless. Embrace this potential and embark on this journey of understanding, healing, and profound connection, filled with hope, optimism, and an unwavering belief in the human spirit's limitless possibilities.

Printed in Great Britain
by Amazon

34069243R00096